AFRICAN AMERICAN MUSIC

A Philosophical Look at African American Music In Society

NATHAN DAVIS
(with a chapter by Ursula Davis,
Professor of Communications
Penn State University, Behrend College)

Cover Photos: Front Cover—Duke Ellington and Mercer Ellington, 1970. Archive Photos/Frank Driggs Collection.
Back Cover—William Grant Still, Archive Photos.

Cover Design: Wing Ip Ngan

Printed in the United States of America

10 9 8 7

ISBN 0-536-58496-6
BA 1523

PEARSON CUSTOM PUBLISHING
75 Arlington Street, Boston, MA 02116
A Pearson Education Company

Table of Contents

Foreword

This book is a labor of love and is the product of countless hours of research and a lifetime of experiential knowledge. The amount of information assembled under this single cover is staggering, and while much of it has been explored with varying degrees of success by other scholars, it is Nathan's unique training, academic background, and street smarts which allow him to bring fresh and often profound insights to the material. The scope of this book is encyclopedic, dealing with everything from African retentions to blues and rap, from the music of Ellington and Coltrane to the body of African American composers who write in the Westem European art [classical] music tradition. There are copious musical examples and wonderful photographs, and the writing style makes the material accessible to cognoscenti and lay persons alike. The chapter by Professor Ursula Broschke Davis on African American artists and intellectuals in Paris during the 1950s and 1960s is wonderfully written and meticulously researched and comes as a delightful and unexpected bonus. This is a fun book to read—confrontational, evocative, provocative, enlightening, riveting, and full of unexpected twists and turns. My advice is to sit back, read, and enjoy!

David N. Baker
Distinguished Professor of Music and Chairman,
Jazz Department
Indiana University School of Music
Bloomington, Indiana

Acknowledgments

The production of this work represents not only my commitment to African American music but also represents the hard work and commitment of many people. Without their dedication and support, this work would not have been possible. Therefore I would like to acknowledge my gratitude to them. First I would like to thank my wife Ursula Broschke Davis. Ursula not only contributed to the body of this work by producing a brilliant chapter on African Americans in Paris but also has tolerated and continues to love and support me through the hectic schedule and sometimes occasional mood swings of a scholar, composer and recording/performing jazz artist who strives daily to remain a God fearing and decent human being in this hectic, fastpaced and sometimes unfair world of ever changing events. I would like to thank my son Pierre Marc Davis for his love and support and a special thanks to my daughter Joyce N. Davis Florida for their suggestions and insight. I also would like to thank my two graduate assistants, Michelle R. Hammond and Mary Ann Morocco for their research and computer assistance. Their help proved invaluable in the final stages of production of this work.

Nathan Davis
July 1995

1 African American Music

Since its inception, African American music has had an enormous impact on the various musics of the world. Everyone, from gifted European composers like Debussy, Stravinsky, Dvorak, Copeland and Satie to the modern 20th century composers—Cage, Stockhausen, Schoenberg and Penderecki—have been affected by the overwhelming power of African American music, especially jazz.

When I was first approached about writing this book, I decided that if I accepted such an enormous challenge, I would try not to duplicate the excellent work already done on the subject by distinguished scholars such as Eileen Southern in *The Music of Black Americans* (New York: W.W. Norton & Co., 1983), Hildred Roach's *Black American Music: Past and Present, Vol. I* (Florida: Robert E. Krieger Publishing, 1985) and Samuel A. Floyd, Jr.'s *Black Music in the Harlem Renaissance: A Collection of Essays.*

Instead, I wanted to focus my book on the intellectual concepts and developmental aspects of African American music. Since many intellectuals maintain that certain forms (e.g., blues, soul, gospels and rap) of African music are primitive and lack the substance necessary for scholarly research, I realized my efforts would not be without problems.

I began to write this book by researching relevant materials in my own personal library, and the libraries at the University of Pittsburgh and Carnegie-Mellon University. My intent was two-fold: to find out if such a book already existed, and to determine if a work such as mine was needed.

After many hours of diligent research, I finally came across a book by one of my former teachers, the brilliant French musician/scholar/author/composer, Andre Hodier. Without a doubt, his brilliant work *Jazz: Its Evolution and Essence* (New York: Grove 1956; Da Capo, 1975) is one of the most thought-provoking books ever written on the subject. Hodier's ability to challenge the reader's concept of jazz (in all its forms) is exceptional to say the least. With Hodier's philosophical concepts well in hand, I formulated a strategy that would guide me in my attempt to provoke and challenge those interested in the subject of African American music, in much the same way Hodier had done for his jazz readers.

An important element of African American music is aesthetics, particularly in an ethnic context. Aesthetics, according to *Webster's Dictionary* is "a branch of philosophy dealing with beauty and the beautiful." In order to understand African American culture as an art form, musical styles—inherent in blues, gospels, jazz, funk, soul and rock—need to be considered as both beautiful and artistically pleasurable.

Artistically speaking, a particular style of ethnic music might be categorized as more pleasurable than another and, depending on the goals of the researcher, certain elements of that style might be assigned a set of values that fit the desired outcome. If this is possible, does the preconceived notion of beauty hold any aesthetic validity? The answer is there is no guarantee that anything categorized as beautiful is, in fact, so. I am certain that African slaves initially did not find the music of their European captors beautiful. According to most historians, the majority of slaves were confused by, and to some degree, insensitive to Western European music. (Given the situation in which they found themselves, an acceptance and appreciation of Western European music was the least of their concerns.)

Beauty is perceived in the context of a particular society, and in the case of ethnic music, as it pertains to a specific cultural group within that society. For example, in certain "primitive" societies, physical beauty is linked to the number of ornaments inserted into portions of the body, i.e., the insertion of animal bones or similar objects into the ear lobes or nose. In the case of the African slave, the concept of beauty was shaped and nurtured by the artistic forms of dance, art (in the form of sculpture, sketching, acting and wood carving) and storytelling. Beauty then, as in any art form, depends on perception, history, customs, attitude and philosophy.

What is art? Who determines the validity of art? Where does art come from? Who is the rightful owner/caretaker of the art form? Can art be learned or transferred to someone outside the immediate culture? These questions must be answered in order to understand a particular culture. These questions have plagued the various forms of African American music since its beginnings, thus causing generations of scholars to inaccurately interpret the essence of African American music. Even today, this miscarriage of "artistic justice" exists; African American music (such as jazz, gospel music and certain forms of blues) is still evaluated by applying Western European musical standards (i.e., form, rhythm, tuning, phrasing, scales, modes). In fact, critics who wrote about jazz during its nascent stage (early 1900s) applied Western European standards to an obviously non-Western music and contributed to undermining the artistic integrity of the music. (The question of integrity in music and other similar issues will be considered in a later chapter.)

The history of African American music dates back to 1619 with the arrival of the African slave in the North American colonies. Slavery not only provided the colonies of France, England, Spain, Holland, Portugal, Germany, etc. with a source of cheap labor but also set the stage for a cultural experiment that has not been duplicated. The cultural exchange that took place on plantations, villages and towns occurred between slaves and masters, between indentured Africans, native Americans or Asians and Western European masters. (It is interesting that the plight of Asian slaves has been overlooked by historians.)

African trade with China and other Asian nations during the Middle Ages (eighth to fourteenth centuries) set the stage for a mutual exchange of culture, language, art and music. ("The Afro-American Musical Legacy to 1800," Robert Stevenson, *The Music Quarterly*). The limited modes of transportation at this time also facilitated cultural exchange, because traders, unable to return home immediately upon completion of their business, instead, remained for a considerable length of time in the host country. During their stay (which in some instances lasted for several months) it is likely that they were entertained by the cultural presentations, dances and songs that may have been part of any celebrations or festivities that took place.

The extent of the cultural exchange must be examined in order to understand the culture of a particular region. The assumption that only the dominant culture is worthy of thorough examination is absurd since the degree of the exchange, by either a dominant or subordinate culture, is relevant and has an impact on the final result. As "cultural" scientists, our first responsibility is to research accurately every facet of a particular art form.

2 A Case for African American Music

During the 1960s, I questioned the validity of musical education (historical musicology, ethnomusicology, performance, composition) as it was being taught in academia. While universities, colleges and music conservatories appreciated African music (jazz, blues, gospels, work songs, game songs, folk songs, rhythm & blues, soul, fusion, funk), academics did not view it as a serious or viable course of study. Until Melvin J. Herskovits' *The Myth of the Negro Past* (Beacon Press) and later Alan Lomax's *Folk Song Style and Culture* (American Association for the Advancement of Science), little, if any, serious research had been done on African American music, and European scholars had focused on African rather than African American culture, perhaps because they found the prospect of studying a strange almost surrealistic music intriguing but not intellectually compelling.

According to Leroi Jones, author of *Blues People* (William Morrow and Co.), slaves maintained an African cultural tradition for their first fifty to one hundred years in North America even while adapting to the traditions and customs of the colonists. The adoption of a foreign culture occurred simultaneously with the retention of the traditional culture, eventually giving birth to a unique, different, yet similar culture. Thus African American culture was born.

The arrival of the African slave in 1619 was the beginning of what most music scholars refer to as the cross-fertilization period, or (in the case of African American music) the coming together of Western European and Western African music in North America. The coming together of these two great forms of music was the first step in the colonies toward the final "melange" that produced the African American music of spirituals, gospels, blues, jazz, etc.

Often overlooked is the enormous amount of cross-fertilization that took place in Africa—before slaves were captured, sold and transported to the colonies. It was the Africans who first enslaved their own people and who in many instances sold, traded and placed them in the hands of the Europeans. "In Dahomey, for example, a kingdom on the Guinea coast which extended from its port, Whydah, some 150 miles into the interior, the annual 'war' operated to

Watercolor of slave ship Albatross by Geoffrey Meynall. Copyright © National Maritime Museum Picture Library.

supply the slave dealers" (*The Myth of the Negro Past,* M. J. Herskovits pg. 35). As Olly Wilson amply explains,

> there existed in each of the African nations represented in the slave trade various cultural differences, languages, dance, music etc., and this does not even take into consideration the fact that there exist what I called 'micro cultural cells' even within these national and tribal units. (*The Relationship of Afro-American Music to West African Music,* p. 2, Olly Wilson)

In addition there exists the question of the various religions and their effect on African, and subsequently African American, music. One of the most important nonindigenous musics to play an important role in the development of African American music is the music of Islam. According to Professor K. Nketia,

"So far as Islam acted as a carrier of Arabic musical traditions, the extent of the change that can be attributed to it varies considerably—from areas in which Islamic conquest was complete, both culturally and politically, to areas in which Islamic agents provided services but failed to conquer or convert to Islam." (*Essays on Music and History in Africa,* ed. by K. Wachsmann, Northwestern University Press, "History and Organization of Music in West Africa," p. 22).

For Professor Nketia, Islam represented only one source of musical change in the "grand melange" of cultures. There is the larger question of the relationship that existed between the African slave and the Western European captor.

The cultural integration of English, French, Dutch, Danes, Portuguese, Spanish and Germans, presented an even more complicated scenario (African Civilisation in the New World, Roger Bastide, Harper and Row, pp. 5–7). But to understand the full cultural implications of the cross-fertilization of these cultures, it would be necessary to study all of the African countries and European nations involved in the slave trade and the roles each played in the settling of the colonies. (*Folk and Traditional Music of Western Continents,* Bruno Nettl, Prentice-Hall).

Another point of concern is that the majority of these studies refer to the African slaves as one people—the African slave. However, these same scholars frequently refer to the various European colonial powers by individual countries (e.g., as the French, Dutch, British). This lack of scholarly precision tends to overlook the differences that existed within Africa, such as the difference between Dahomians and Ghanaians or between Nigerians and Senegalese, thus omitting a multitude of cultural differences such as languages, both tribal and regional, dances, religious beliefs, tribal songs, etc. As we study the similarities between Western European and Western African cultures, it is also important to examine their differences.

3 African Retentions

Once the mixing of European and African cultures in North America has been studied, the next issue to examine is the phenomena of change and retention during the long ordeal of slavery. Some scholars believe that very little pure African culture survived the rigorous pressures brought about as a result of the enslavement of West Africans in North America.

"Scholarly opinion presents a fairly homogeneous conception as to African survivals in the United States. On the whole, specialists tend to accept and stress the view that some Africanisms may have disappeared as a result of the pressures exerted by the experience of slavery on all aboriginal modes of thought or behavior." (Herskovits, Beacon Press, p. 3)

According to Leroi Jones *(Blues People),* the process of Africanisation—the changing from Africanism to Afro-Americanism—took place in the 1700s and 1800s. This cross-fertilization, the act of assimilating the various forms of fragmented African cultures with the diversified forms of European cultures, was the first step in the construction of a purely new and indigenous music—African American music. African American music then is a combination of predominately Western African, Western European, native American Indian, and to a lesser degree Asian, music.

Perhaps one of the most overlooked cultural contributions to the development of African American music is that of the American Indians. As a youngster growing up in Kansas City, I found myself surrounded with both real and imaginative American Indian cultural folklore. Stories of indigenous Indians, African and African American cultural and social exchanges were rampant. jazz bassist Charlie Mingus and Oscar Petiford both claim American Indian cultural and racial heritage.

While researching music on the French West Indian islands of Martinique and Guadeloupe in 1974, I became involved with a group of cultural anthropologists and musicians who primarily were interested in the music and social habits of the Amerindians, particularly the "Carib-Noir." The term Carib-Noir refers to a racial mixture of African and Caribbean Indians who lived in the Caribbean islands and were the children of slaves who were shipwrecked during the early years of the slave trade. Many of these slaves were adopted by

Charlie Mingus. Archive Photos/Frank Driggs Collection.

various Amerindian tribes and were eventually accepted as official members of the tribe; in many instances, they even rose to become chiefs of the tribe. Many intermarried, producing a completely different race—the Amerindians.

Needless to say, the slaves also brought with them their original indigenous music and culture. The exchange between African American slaves and the Amerindians produced a foreign yet related culture. In fact, within the African American community it was prestigious to have American Indian "blood" or any other ethnic connection. This embracing of another culture may have been a psychological attempt to escape the atrocities of slavery. The American Indian, who in many instances proved himself unsuitable for the hard physical labor associated with slavery, was eventually used as a guide or messenger.

Most historians agree that the mixing of Indians and Africans was more prevalent in the Caribbean and Latin America than in the U.S. But strong evidence also points to a more involved acculturation process between the two

Garifuna: A mixture of island Carib and African, the Garifuna originally arrived in Belize in 1802. They migrated from St. Vincent and the Grenadines, Caribbean islands. Each year they celebrate their settlement day on November 19th, but early records date their first major settlement to 1832. Photo, courtesy of the Belize Information Service and Caribbean Heritage Magazine.

groups in the U.S. than previously thought. Indeed, an in-depth study conducted among African Americans to determine the degree to which Africans and Amerindians or Native American Indians mixed, might indicate that at least one quarter of the African slaves in the United States intermingled with native Indians.

This intermingling can be seen in areas of the south like Mississippi and Oklahoma. In my own family, according to interviews with my grandmother, our ancestors intermingled with the Cherokee and Blackfoot Indians (as well as with German Jews). Since the advent of Alex Haley's book *Roots,* numerous African Americans have begun to research their family history, providing information that clearly verifies the strong interaction that took place between the indigenous Amerindians and the African slaves.

4 The European Connection

A significant number of scholars and laymen agree that in the case of African American music, the most important cultural cross-fertilization took place between Western Europeans and Western Africans. In the U.S., the adaptation, acculturation and transformation of Western European religious music, game songs, brass bands, folk songs, orchestra music and operas resulted in music that was later called jazz, gospels, spirituals and work songs.

A close examination of these various forms of African and African American music yields the extent of this cultural marriage. It is virtually impossible to deny the close bond that exists between Western African music and Western European religious music. The very existence of spirituals and other forms of African American religious music attests to this link because original African religions did not contain any reference to biblical figures such as Joshua, Moses, or even Jesus. These names, as well as the spirituality they represented, were learned only when the African slave arrived on the plantation. According to John Hope Franklin in his work *From Slavery to Freedom:*

> The religion of the early Africans can most accurately be described as ancestor worship. The Africans believed that the spirits of their forefathers had unlimited power over their lives. (p. 31)

Therefore, an analysis of the roots of African religions requires an understanding of its tribal and regional heritage.

> Traditional religions are not universal: they are tribal or national. Each religion is bound and limited to the people among whom it has evolved. One traditional religion cannot be propagated in another tribal group. This does not rule out the fact that religious ideas may spread from one people to another. But such ideas spread spontaneously, especially through migrations, intermarriage, conquest, or expert knowledge being sought by individuals of one tribal group from another. Traditional religions have no missionaries to propagate them; and one individual does not preach his religion to another. (*African Religions and Philosophy,* by John S. Mbiti, p. 5, Anchor Books, Doubleday and Co., Garden City, NY)

However, what makes a particular style of music African or African American is not only the music but also the style or manner in which the music is performed. Gospels, spirituals and jazz are learned musical responses based on a multi-diversified African culture; they are reinterpretations (and in the case of Western European music, adaptations) of already-existing cultural forms. The blues (or any other form of African American music) can be performed in a non-blues manner, and the same is true for gospels or spirituals (gospels or spirituals can also be performed in a style completely foreign to its original intent). Some examples of so-called bluesy or jazzy versions of traditional non-African American music can be seen in Ray Charles' recording of the American patriotic song "America" (God Bless America) or Fats Domino's rendition of the classic "Blueberry Hill."

The effect of Western European religion on the music and culture of African slaves cannot be overestimated. Even today, the effect of religion on world culture is evident, e.g., the conflicts in Northern Ireland between Catholics and Protestants and in the Middle East between Israel and the Palestinians. These and other similar conflicts help change the course of history. Religion is one of, if not the most, powerful forces responsible for shaping world events and influencing thought. Its role in the cultural transformation of the African slave cannot be underestimated .

According to writer and scholar Leroi Jones, "Christianity was adopted by Negroes before the great attempts by missionaries and evangelists in the early part of the nineteenth century to convert them." (Jones, *Blues People,* p. 33) Jones attributes this acceptance of Christianity to the slaves' experience during the early stages of slavery in the colonies. Traditional African religions were not permitted because colonists were reluctant to allow slaves to continue practicing a religion that was culturally foreign to the religions of Western Europeans.

Religion also had an impact on the African slaves' acceptance of Western European music. Cut off from the music and other aspects of cultural heritage, the slave had no other choice but to embrace whatever spiritual substitute he found, i.e., European music. Whereas Western European culture first served as a substitute for their own culture, it later took on a cultural life of its own, by contributing to the various forms of the new music—African American music. The total effect of this changing as a result of the process of cross-fertilization will be examined in a more thorough manner in a later chapter.

According to Bruno Nettl in his book *Folk and Traditional Music of the Western Continent* (pp. 52–54, Prentice Hall), there exist various types and styles of Western European music, including epics, ballads, love songs, ceremonial songs, spirituals, folk songs, children's songs, humorous songs, work songs and dance songs. The European countries that Nettl refers to include, but are not limited to, Spain, England, France and Germany, and each of these countries or nationalities was involved to some degree in the exchange of culture that resulted from the slave trade.

As responsible researchers, our task is to determine how much of a particular song form or dance is derived from European culture and how much can be attributed to the Western African's own culture. Some scholars may argue that the degree or size of the contribution from one particular group is irrelevant, but political fallout (e.g., the question of who is responsible for the development of jazz, gospels, etc., in the U.S.) requires an examination of the degree of contribution by each group.

One factor to consider is the degree of contact that existed between the two groups, in this case, the group of French, German, Italians, Spanish, and others on various plantations in the U.S. From various historical accounts, we know that these European groups were involved in the daily lives of their slaves. This suggests that everything, from language to the eating habits, was governed or determined by the dominant culture. So many song forms, once thought to have originated with the slaves, actually were introduced to them by European colonists. However, colonists borrowed as many songs and dances from the slaves as the African slaves did from Western European colonists.

Slaves altered Western European songs to make them special or different, e.g., the Negro spiritual. While many Negro spirituals pay tribute to Jesus, Jericho, Jerusalem and Moses, these songs actually were based on Western European religious concepts and not on any of the numerous African religions. Additional evidence of the African slaves' ability to adapt to and re-define the music of the European can be seen in the following quote by Harold Courlander from his book *Negro Songs from Alabama:*

> Nevertheless, the absorption into 'Negro music' of European elements must have begun at a very early date. In her book *Journal of a Residence on a Georgia Plantation,* describing life in the 1830s, Frances Anne Kemble quoted some songs sung by slaves which (though she believed them to be of Negro invention) were of English derivation." (Oak Publication, NY.)

Work Songs

Together with spirituals, gospels and other religious song forms, work songs formed the basis of African American folk songs. As originally conceived, work songs were designed to help the worker do his work in an easy and efficient manner, and the modern version of the work song can be found today in factories, elevators, hospitals and waiting rooms around the world.

The use of music as an agent in altering or changing human behavior dates back to the beginning of time. (The Mysticism of Sound by Nyatt Khan). For example, slavery (forced free labor furnished by a subordinate group), provides a base for examining the effect of music on labor.

Work songs varied according to the type of work being done. (Davis, *Writings in Jazz,* Kendall Hunt) If the work was picking cotton, a song was created to help the worker with the task at hand. If the work consisted of rowing barges, then the work song took on the character of the sea shanty, a work song used by African oarsmen to help them row from one destination to another. (Sea shanties have been traced from destinations as diverse as New Orleans to Liverpool, England.) Slaves, improvising on material learned from the Europeans, invented songs that enabled them to get through the day's work.

Perhaps the most important ingredient found in the work song is its rhythm. A chain gang leader who could set the correct rhythm and inspired

Convicts working on the quarry rock pile 1/2-mile from America's toughest prison in Georgia, 1919. The Bettmann Archive.

his workers to give their best was in great demand and was a highly prized possession. Throughout African American history, the folktales of chain-gang leaders like John Henry are legendary. "John Henry could out-work and out-sing any man on the gang," and his ability as a chain-gang leader was accredited to his flawless sense of rhythm. (*The Negro in Making of America,* by Benjamin Quarles Collier, Macmillan Publishers, p. 30).

Even today, the work song cannot be overestimated in the modern workplace. Piped-in music in factories throughout the world attests to the importance of music as a force that stimulates workers to complete their tasks. In most cases, the psychological effect of soothing music, surrounding the work place with a kind of spiritual mystical ambiance, provides just the right climate for accomplishing the job at hand.

5 Africanization

The process of Africanization—the changing of the results of the process of cross-fertilization—is responsible, in part, for what has been called the "black sound." Just what is a black sound, or as it was referred to earlier, Negroid sound?

Negroid sound, as it was described by early scholars, was attributed to cultural factors such as texture, language, speech and pronunciation, and the tonal relationship of language and sound. In other words the first concept of sound, and eventually music, is based on the sounds first heard as an infant. In fact, there is a school of thought that considers the best way to insure a child is musical is to play recorded sounds for the pregnant mother, thus acclimating the child to music even before birth.

Sound is the basis of music and the production of sound is as much a part of music making as rhythm or melody. The question of an authentic Black or Negroid sound continues to surface even today whenever musicologists or ethnomusicologists discuss African American music such as blues, gospels and certain authentic forms of jazz. (Certain styles of jazz—swing, hard bop, avant-garde—represent the harder swinging, rougher sounds of jazz compared to the more subtle styles like cool or third stream jazz.)

Theoretically, in the case of African American music, the interval of a minor third was responsible in part for the blues-like sonority associated with the Negroid sound. Ethnomusicologists like A. M. Jones and Hughes Tracy agree that the lowered third and the lowered seventh appeared to be prevalent in the majority of the African music studied. The seemingly downward thrust suggested by the lowered third produces the "blue" feeling that is associated with blues. The same "blue" feeling is evident in many forms of African American religious music.

The process of changing whatever the slaves came in contact with was a form of self preservation and was common practice by all slaves. It is doubtful there was any conscious effort or plan by the slaves to create something new. Thus the creative genius that developed from this process was a natural, rather than planned, process.

The Universality of Spirituality

I once spoke to a good friend and Ghanaian colleague, Komala Amoaku (a master drummer from Ghana and a graduate of the University of Pittsburgh with a Ph.D. in Ethnomusicology) about the art of building an African drum for our newly formed African drum ensemble. He informed me that the first step would be to select a special tree located at a special place and to pray and bless both the plot of land and the tree before cutting down the tree. He also told me that if the proper ritual were not followed, the drum would never have the proper sound. Later, I spoke to another colleague, Dr. Fela Sowande, professor of ethnomusicology at the University of Pittsburgh, who confirmed Komala's statement that in order to build a drum, one must first select the proper space and then bless both the space and the tree before cutting it down. Fela added that if this was not done properly, the particular drum would never sound well, regardless of the performer's ability.

This inside look at the concept of spirituality often is overlooked by the outsider (someone born outside of the culture) who is unfamiliar with the prevailing culture. It is important to realize that this "unseen" spirituality existed in other aspects of African life, such as dance, story telling and woodcarving. This same spirituality carried over into the music of the blues, jazz, spirituals, gospels, game songs, etc.

Spirituality also suggests a Midas touch (the mythological legend of King Midas who was able to turn everything he touched into gold), because this changing of everything the African slave laid his/her hands on is a major factor in understanding the African slaves' approach to survival in the new world. This process of Africanization, the changing of the results of cross-fertilization, is the ingredient most overlooked when critics discuss the origins of jazz and other forms of African American music.

6 Afro-Linguistics and Music

A Case for Afro-Linguistics (as it relates to music)

The impact of Afro-linguistics on the music of African Americans cannot be underestimated. Without the use of special attacks, voice inflections and the changing of rhythmical implications, African American music would not have developed as it has. This is especially noticeable when someone from outside the African American culture attempts to imitate the African American style of singing. The performer's success depends on a familiarity with the lifestyle, cultural background and music of the African Americans. Performers who have studied the language systematically, observed the dance and movements, and have an affinity for the overall lifestyle, tend to be more successful than those who have not had such experiences.

The key words here are experience and familiarity. It is not simply a matter of race that determines whether someone can perform successfully in an African American style; rather, success depends more on the above-mentioned cultural elements.

It can be detected easily when an instrumentalist or vocalist does not phrase or pronounce a word correctly. When listening to an instrumentalist like Louis Armstrong or Charlie Parker, however, we can hear the resemblance of the phrasing used by a good jazz instrumentalist, especially if we translate vocal sounds into nonvocal concepts. For instance, if Louis Armstrong sings "dat there" or "dare" we must translate the "dat there" into musical terms. This translation depends on the attack and the "scooping" or the "dining and wining" of the notes involved. "Scooping or dining and wining" of the notes refers to the technique of not directly playing the note in tune; instead, the note is approached from a semi-tone below. This technique, one of many used in jazz, produces the desired effects of color and feeling. In jazz as well as classical music, instrumental music is a representation of vocal music or the human voice. Many great jazz instrumentalists, e.g., Miles Davis and Lester Young, tended to pattern their musical styles and sounds after great jazz vocalists like Billie Holiday; basically, these musicians tried to make their instruments "sing."

A study of the effect of language on the music of any culture presents a very exciting and challenging prospect and can change the way we look at music in society. Such a research project would require the careful reexamination of the various dialects spoken during slavery. These dialects, and the tribes who spoke them, would have to be traced to the primary geographic area and/or plantations where they were first spoken. Other aspects to consider are: (1) the linguistic influences of the speech patterns, and (2) the dialect of the various slave owners. For example, a Nigerian slave, sold to an Englishman from Georgia, then traded to a French plantation owner in Louisiana, presents a different set of challenges than a slave who had been sold by a Dutch farmer to a Spanish-speaking farmer in Florida. However outlandish these theories may seem, they are a reality.

One of the most fascinating aspects of studying the slave trade is reenacting the journey of the slave—from captivity in Africa, through his journey across the Atlantic, to the various plantations in the Americas, and finally to freedom. Many changes, both physical and social, occurred during this sojourn including illness, death, spiritual, psychological and physical trauma, as well as changes within the socio-political structure of the group.

In the Kansas City area where I spent my youth, it was assumed that the various ways of pronouncing certain words actually stemmed from a combination of German, Spanish and English. The degree of influence these languages had on the resulting dialect spoken in the Kansas City area has never been determined. However, during my youth, I can remember hearing blues singers with an accent that sounded considerably different from the singing I had heard in other parts of the country, particularly songs I listened to when I visited my grandmother in Mississippi. Perhaps somewhere in the historical development of these singers the difference in these dialects can be attributed to an African slave who had been enslaved by a different tribe in his native Africa and eventually sold to a Spanish- or French-speaking slave owner in the colonies.

If we learn to hear music as a result of first hearing the sounds that surround us as an infant—a mother's tender voice, the noise of a rattle, the cry of a sibling and other sounds around us during our first hours immediately following birth—then these sounds obviously play an important role in shaping our concept of music. Of these sounds, it is the sound of the mother's voice that most interests us as musical scientists.

We learn to hear music, especially sounds that are the foundation of music, by imitating the sounds we first hear as infants. In many societies these first sounds are attributed to the mother's voice. These primary sounds form the subconscious basis of our future reference regarding music. These preliminary sounds, over a period of time, become a subconscious tonal reference that is subsequently referred to whenever we hear music. In his book *The Mysticism of Sound* (International Sufi organization), Hazrat Nyatt Kahn states that each of us has a naturally built-in sound that is germane to our individual body rhythms. He further suggests that in order to find our "natural sound" we have only to sit quietly and breath deeply in a controlled rhythm, quietly listening for the dominating sonority produced by our breathing. The emerging sound is the "natural sound" of our body.

I have experimented with this eclectic, spiritual exercise and did indeed produce an overall sonority that sounded in tune with my body's natural rhythm. So if, in fact, we all have a special sonority that is particular to our bodies, it would appear that this intuitive process is the same process we refer to when we first begin to learn the meaning of sound and eventually music.

In the case of the first African slaves, this process took place in Africa and occurred at the breast of an African speaking mother. These sounds, according to Kahn's theory of intuitive sound, were responsible for shaping the tonal reference of the infant. Therefore, the concept of a 'cultural sound', or a sound that is directly related to a particular cultural group, would be African in the case of the early slaves, and would reflect the tonal language of the particular African dialect spoken by the elders.

In his book Black English (Vintage Books–Random House, New York, p. 84), author J.L. Dillard outlines three different types of English that was spoken on the plantation: "Evidence such as these advertisements seems to establish that by the early part of the eighteenth century, at least three varieties of English were in use by Negroes in the thirteen colonies": West African Pidgin English, Plantation Creole and Standard English. Dillard further states: "The differentiation of varieties of English used by black speakers, based most probably upon social factors within the slave community, is evident by the early eighteenth century."

The fact is there were a number of subdifferentiations that emerged from these three major types. One of these sublanguages was Gullah. Gullah, according to Fred McNeese in an article entitled "Helping Hand For Black English," *Black English* was a language dating back to slavery days. It combines English with elements of various African languages. McNeese, who interviewed John Gadson Sr. (Director of the Sea Island Language Project at Beaufort, S.C.) states "its (Black English's) influence is so strong among blacks on the coast near the Georgia/South Carolina line that 75 percent of them have difficulty writing and speaking standard English." He further states that Gullah also is noted for its deletion of reference to the sex of the subject being discussed. For example, "um" is substituted for such pronouns as his and her, where "um go outside" is used instead of "he goes outside" and "um" replaces the word he.

If the word "um" were used in a blues phrase instead of the word he, the feeling of the phrase, both linguistically and musically, would change completely. The pronoun *he* is a lower or more masculine sounding word when compared to um, which has a higher sound and produces a more feminine feeling. The reason then, that blues sounds the way it does, is because of the use of such words as um, dem, dey, dos, gwine, bes, etc.

When we examine the enormous impact these sublanguages may have had on the early creators of African American music, we can understand the real "roots" of jazz, blues, gospels and other forms of this great music. Indeed, through the use of music forms such as blues, jazz, spirituals and gospels, the African American has succeeded in changing the way in which the English language is spoken all over the world.

During my early years living in Europe (mainly in Paris) as a freelance jazz musician, I was always amazed at the fascination European jazz fans had with the way I spoke English, particularly the British, who frequently asked me to repeat certain phrases so they could learn to say them the way I did—with the "proper Kansas City twang" or accent. Because they were deeply committed jazz fans, they tried on many occasions to sound like me, using the same inflections and nuances that I used.

7 Duke Ellington and His Contemporaries

Background

As a young African American child growing up in the Midwest (Kansas City), I often found myself feeling inferior; not only to the few remaining non-African-American youngsters in our neighborhood, but also to my fellow African American playmates. The reason for this inferiority was primarily because of my interest in jazz. Early in life, I had become interested in the music of Duke Ellington, Coleman Hawkins, Illinois Jacquet, and Louis Jordan while listening to the many records my father had and to the records played for me by my neighbor, Rev. Kid, a Methodist minister. But my interest in jazz was viewed by the other kids as odd, which in itself was "bizarre" since none of the other kids (or their parents), black or white, even knew who Duke Ellington was. Because of his enormous popularity (attributed more to his ability as a showman rather than to his talent as a musician), Louis Jordan was at least known by some of my friends.

As I approached high school, the situation deteriorated. Virtually none of my fellow students and relatively few of my teachers, with the exception of my high school band director and mentor, Mr. Robert N. Clarke, really knew anything about Duke Ellington or his music. Only a handful of the so-called educated parents and a few of the teachers would admit that they used to dance to Duke's songs, *It don't mean a thing if it aint got that swing and Take the 'A' train.* The fact that the majority of the world considered Duke Ellington to be one of, if not the most, important American composers in history was ignored or simply not known. I must confess that I too was unaware of Ellington's worldwide reputation renown before traveling to various European capital cities as a member of the University of Kansas variety show, "Jay Hawke Jamboree." In my own defense, however, most teenagers in the U.S. during the 1950s, regardless of race, were unfamiliar with Duke Ellington.

At the height of his musical accomplishments, Duke Ellington was an African American in a society that overlooked the achievements of many African Americans, musical or otherwise; his exclusion from the cultural elite of American society highlights this problem (here I am referring to his earlier life in Washington D.C.). Ellington's talents also went unrecognized (at least to the degree that other American composers of similar abilities were recognized) because his music, jazz, was not exposed to the music world at the same level as his Euro-American counterparts.

Historically, jazz was considered a "renegade music" and was not accepted in the same circles of society as Western European art (classical) music, regardless of whether it was performed by African Americans or European Americans. Yet the audience for jazz music, particularly jazz as a dance music, played an important role in the integration of jazz into the musical mainstream.

Ellington played a sophisticated type of dance music. But during the 1920's, in the Midwest and other areas outside the Northeast, his music was considered by many jazz purists to be "too hard to dance to"; Bennie Moten, Andy Kirk's "Clouds of Joy" and Jimmy Lunceford all were considered better dance bands. However, as Ken Rattenbury states in his book *Duke Ellington Jazz Composer,* "before anyone else in jazz, Duke Ellington accomplished a genuine, methodical integration of black folk-music practices with white urban ones." In fact, Ellington bridged the gap between the sophisticated, quasiclassical jazz style of the East and the rougher, blues-oriented dance styles prevalent in the Midwest and South.

Ellington was an extremely intelligent observer of human nature who had the gift of learning from every encounter and experience he had. As Ken Rattenbury states: "Through his own dedicated, personal effort and acute powers of aural observation—through the acts of writing and presenting his works—he chronicled the development of jazz at a critical stage."

To further understand the depth of Ellington's work and its relationship to other great composers of European music, consider a quote from composer Constant Lambert in *The Negro in American Culture* by Margaret Just Butcher:

> Ellington is . . . a real composer, the first composer of distinction and the first Negro composer of distinction. . . . I know of nothing in Ravel so dexterous in treatment as the varied solos in the middle of the ebullient *Hot and Bothered* and nothing in Stravinsky more dynamic than the final section. (p. 68)

Gunther Schuller in his brilliant work entitled *Early Jazz* (Oxford University Press) states:

> Duke Ellington is one of America's great composers. At this writing his extraordinary creativity seems undiminished. In looking over more than forty years of his career, we can only marvel at the consistency with which Ellington and his orchestra have sustained a level of inspiration comparable in its way to that of the major 'classical' composers of our century. (p. 318).

To comprehend the music of Duke Ellington, it is first necessary to understand the way he thought about music and life. His suave, polished manner was shaped by his mother, Daisy Kennedy Ellington, and his father James Edward Ellington. According to music historian John Edward Hasse in his book *Beyond Category, The Life and Genius of Duke Ellington* (Simon & Schuster),

Duke Ellington. Archive Photos/Frank Driggs Collection.

Duke Ellington was born April 29, 1899 in Washington, D.C., into an upper middle class Negro family (pp. 21–25). According to Ellington himself, he was a pampered and spoiled child. His mother and sister, Ruth, literally worshipped the ground he walked on. Both his parents provided him with a positive role model that gave Ellington a strong sense of security and, in some instances, a superior attitude toward life.

Duke worshipped both his parents; "as Edward adored and even worshipped his mother, he admired his father." (*Beyond Category,* Hasse, p. 24). His immaculate ways and seemingly unlimited sense of charm were learned from his father; his strong commitment to racial pride and undeniable quest for perfection were acquired from his mother.

According to African American sociologist, Kenneth Clarke, "The Black Bourgeois" always had regarded Washington, D.C. as the center of black culture in the U.S. The term "the upper 400s" refers to a group of elite African Americans who felt superior to less fortunate African Americans who had not reached a certain level of social and economic stability.

This particular kind of social division is in many ways similar to the division that existed between Creoles and blacks in early New Orleans during the 1800 and 1900s. In New Orleans, the division was based primarily on shades of skin color. Lighter skinned "Negroes," primarily the descendants of French or Spanish fathers and African mothers, considered themselves superior to blacker-skinned Negroes who were the descendants both of African mothers and African fathers.

This same interracial phenomenon also was evident in the nation's capital. In Washington, D.C., skin color was important but proximity to the seat of political power played an equally important role. Even African Americans who were not employed by the government, but worked in menial, related jobs as caterers, janitors and domestics, felt superior to other blacks because they were close to the seat of political power. John Edward Hasse states: "The poet Langston Hughes was harshly critical of Washington's Negro society. "Never before, anywhere," he wrote:

> had I seen persons of influence—men with some money, women with some beauty, teachers with some education—quite so audibly sure of their own importance and their high places in the community. So many pompous gentlemen never before did I meet. (p. 32, *Beyond Category*)

This statement verifies the extent to which the bourgeois social climate played a role in shaping Ellington's perspective on life. What may have been a superior attitude toward life was, in fact, a profound sense of self worth. Ellington had been told all his life that he was special, and he was. His commitment to perfection, beauty and elegance in his music was a result of his upbringing.

Duke's suave, polished manners served him well later in his life. Because of his amiable personality and legendary stature as a musician, he was in constant demand by the U.S. government as a representative of "the American way of life"; in fact, he was the first jazz musician to be given the title of America's "unofficial diplomat." Ellington frequently acted an ambassador of good will during his overseas tours, doing what he did best—performing his music—and presenting the government in a positive light. Many heads of state in countries Ellington visited were jazz fans, and Duke's performances served to lessen the tension, if and when it existed, between the U.S. and a particular country. His success in this capacity caused the government to use more jazz artists for this purpose. (For further information on the use of jazz and African American music by the U.S. as a diplomatic tool see *Black Nationalism and Revolution in Music,* by Frank Kofsky).

Ellington the Cultural Activist

In many ways, Duke Ellington was a cultural activist. As an African American male, he never acknowledged the indecent innuendoes associated with racial discrimination; he was too proud and too well educated to do so. Instead, he would "anoint" the situation with a special Ellington phrase, gracefully letting the perpetrator know that he or she was "out of line." Without the social grace and diplomacy, inherited from his father, Duke may not have been as effective as a statesman.

Ellington's somewhat superior attitude toward less fortunate blacks partially can be attributed to his desire to escape the realities of racial prejudice. However, careful examination of his music in *Creole Rhapsody,* parts 1 and 2

(1931), *Creole Love Call* (1927), Black and Tan Fantasy (1927), *Sweet Chariot* (late 1930), and *Black, Brown and Beige* (1944), shows that Duke, indeed, was proud to be an African American as well as an American. Although he acknowledged the existence of racial prejudice in the U.S., Ellington refused to let it make him bitter; he preferred instead to attribute such uncivilized behavior to the shortcomings of the individual rather than to an entire race.

Perhaps the one thing that becomes obvious when listening to Ellington's work, from the standpoint of orchestration, is his ability to weave together a cushion of sound that is both lush and yet at the same time hauntingly fluid and, to a certain degree, penetrating. This can be seen in example R.A.-I. Ellington accomplishes this effect by first using an unusual layer of instruments which include: clarinet; soprano sax; alto sax and finally baritone sax. The baritone sax plays a pivotal role by stating its own melody and yet, at the same time, remaining an integral part of the overall harmonic scheme.

R. A. I Concert Reduction
Duke Ellington's *Subtle Lament*

The voicing is brilliant, particularly since the date of composition was March 20, 1939 (according to transcriber David Berger). The first two chords of section A, measure 1, represent the harmonic concept (the utilization of 4th's) associated with players from much later periods (e.g., 1960's–1980's). For example, by voicing the F# (the third degree) in the bottom of the chord and placing the next note a minor 5th above:

followed by an E (which is a "tight" 3rd) and finally completing the chord by voicing the B (or 6th) at the top of the chord, gives it a modern 1960's sound and feel.

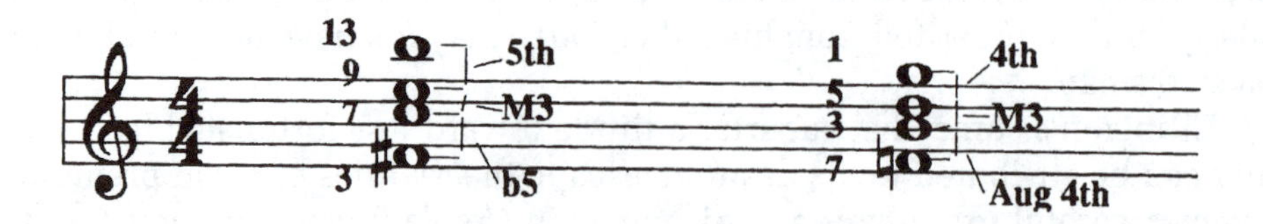

This is even more significant and spectacular when we consider that Ellington never really was thought of as a "Post-Modernist." The genius of Ellington is quite evident when we examine his choice of instruments and the placement of those instruments. By mixing soprano sax with trumpet, alto and baritone sax, he produces a beautiful and light sound possessing an almost vocal quality.

Another quality which Ellington so beautifully displays is the usage of what I call the "extra player" or "space factor." Ellington utilized space as though it were an "extra player" in the orchestra. Space became an integral part of his overall compositional approach and a key player in his total melodic and harmonic concept. This use of silence gave Ellington the ability to fill up the sound without overwriting.

The Music of Duke Ellington

Perhaps the most outstanding characteristic of Duke Ellington's music is its personalized sound. (See analysis.) To the untrained listener, Ellington's music is just plain "sweet." *(During my early youth I often heard this term used in describing Duke's music.)* To the listener of the late 1920s and 1930s, his music was that "sophisticated dance-band music from the northeast," i.e., difficult to dance to.

One of my most favorite Ellington compositions is his salute to Shakespeare, *Such Sweet Thunder.* In *The Duke Ellington Reader,* edited by Mark Tucker (Oxford University Press), journalist and African American scholar, Stanley Crouch states:

> Of the thirteen pieces that comprise *Such Sweet Thunder,* the four 'sonnets' are different in mood, orchestration, and rhythm, but have in common, as Ellington scholar Bill Dobbins points out, fourteen phrases of ten notes each, musically mirroring the fourteen lines of iambic pentameter (ten syllables) that make up the literary sonnet Shakespeare favored. (p. 441)

In order to fully understand the essence of the man, Duke Ellington, I would suggest the following works: *The Duke Ellington Reader* edited by Mark Tucker (Oxford University Press); *Music is my Mistress* by Edward Kennedy Ellington (DaCapo paperbacks); *Early Jazz* by Gunther Schuller (Oxford University Press); *Beyond Category: The Life and Genius of Duke Ellington* by John Edward Hasse (Simon and Schuster); and *Duke Ellington, Jazz Composer* by Ken Rattenbury (Yale University Press).

Perhaps one of the most controversial issues surrounding Ellington was his ability as a pianist. This question is amply discussed in Rattenbury's book, *Duke Ellington: Jazz Composer,* where Rattenbury states:

> "Did Duke Ellington's technical limitations as a pianist, particularly noticeable at the beginning of his career (mid to late 1920's) restrict his compositions or, did they enhance them by observing a link with the basic black musical forms of blues and ragtime and their immediate through Europeanized derivatives?" (Rattenbury, p. 28)

Rattenbury's question is one often raised by critics, and it was a question frequently asked during the 1940s by musicians who saw Ellington as an important composer but not an exceptional pianist.

It is important to remember that Duke Ellington was a product of his time—the Harlem Renaissance period—an era that saw many black intellectuals earnestly trying to imitate and incorporate the music of Western Europe into their own works. There were many musicians, especially pianists, who were more proficient technically than Ellington, e.g., Fats Waller and J.P. Johnson; however, keep in mind that Ellington's primary goal was to be a band leader and not a solo pianist. Duke was as interested in duplicating the sound of the great symphonic works of that period, and these goals, together with his natural intuitive urge to become a great jazz musician, must be taken into consideration when evaluating his overall musical contribution.

Given the extent of his work as a composer, the technique Ellington acquired as a pianist was a direct result of the following: (1) playing various types of dance band engagements earlier in his career; and (2) playing through the various motifs and harmonic structures he used while composing. For Ellington, the piano was a means to an end; he used it to familiarize himself with the sounds he wanted to express in his musical compositions. This is in direct contrast to pianists like Art Tatum, Willie "The Lion" Smith and James P. Johnson, who were primarily performers.

A close examination of Ellington's music reveals a definite affinity to classical composers as well as a direct link to the piano style of pianist Thelonius Monk.

SUBTLE LAMENT

Duke Ellington

transcribed by David Berger

Such
Sweet
Thunder

P.O. Box 1802
Ansonia Station
New York, NY 10023

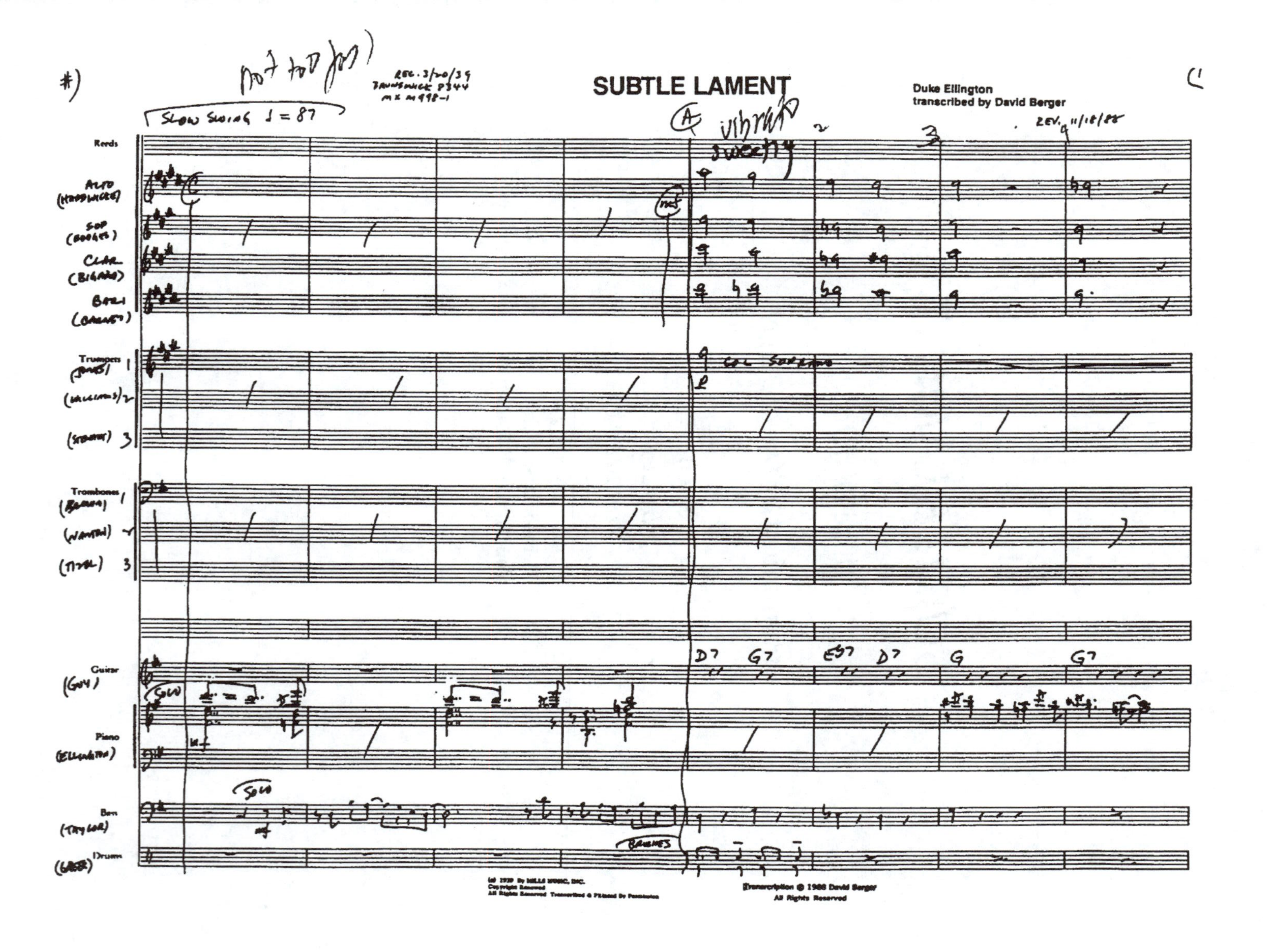
SUBTLE LAMENT
Duke Ellington
transcribed by David Berger
Reeds
Trumpets
Trombones
Guitar
Piano
Bass
Drums
D7 G7 E♭7 D7 G G7
Transcription © 1988 David Berger
All Rights Reserved

Reeds

A

S

C

B

Trumpets 1 2 3

Trombones 1 2 3

Guitar

Piano

Bass

Drums

Cmaj7 C7 | E♭7 D7 | G | G♯o | D7 G7 | E♭7 D7 | G | E♭7 D7

EVEN

Reeds
A
S
T
B
(To TENOR)
Trumpets
Trombones
LAZY
Guitar
D7 G7 Cm6 Eb7 D7 G7 Db C G7 C7 Eb D7 G7 Db D7 G
Piano
Bass
Drums

Reeds
A
S
T
B
TENOR
Trumpets
1
2
3
Trombones
1
2
3
Guitar
D7 G7 Cm6 Eb7 D7 G D7 Ab Cm G D7 G7 Eb7 D7 G7
Piano
Bass
Drums

Reeds
A
S
T
B

Trumpets 1 2 3

D7 F7-9 E7-9 A7 E7 ½ VALVE A7 F7-9 E7-9 A7 NORMAL

mf mf mf

Trombones 1 2 3

½ PLUNGER

Guitar

C7 E♭7 D7 G7 D7 G7 E♭7 D7 G7

Piano

Bass

Drums

D
Reeds
A
S
C
B
Trumpets
Trombones
Guitar
Piano
Drums
D7 G G7 Db C G7 C Fm Bbm Fm Bbm G
Gb7
Fm Bbm Fm Bbm G

Reeds
A
S
C
B
Trumpets
Trombones
Guitar
Piano
Bass
Drums
E
D7 G G7 Db C G7 C Fm Bbm Fm Bbm G
D7 G Cm7 Ab G6 G G7

Reeds
A
S
C
B
Trumpets
Trombones
Guitar
Piano
Bass
Drums
C7 C E♭ A♭ G6 G G7 D7 G7 E♭7 D7 G D7 A7 E♭7 D7 G
RIT
OPEN
COL SOP

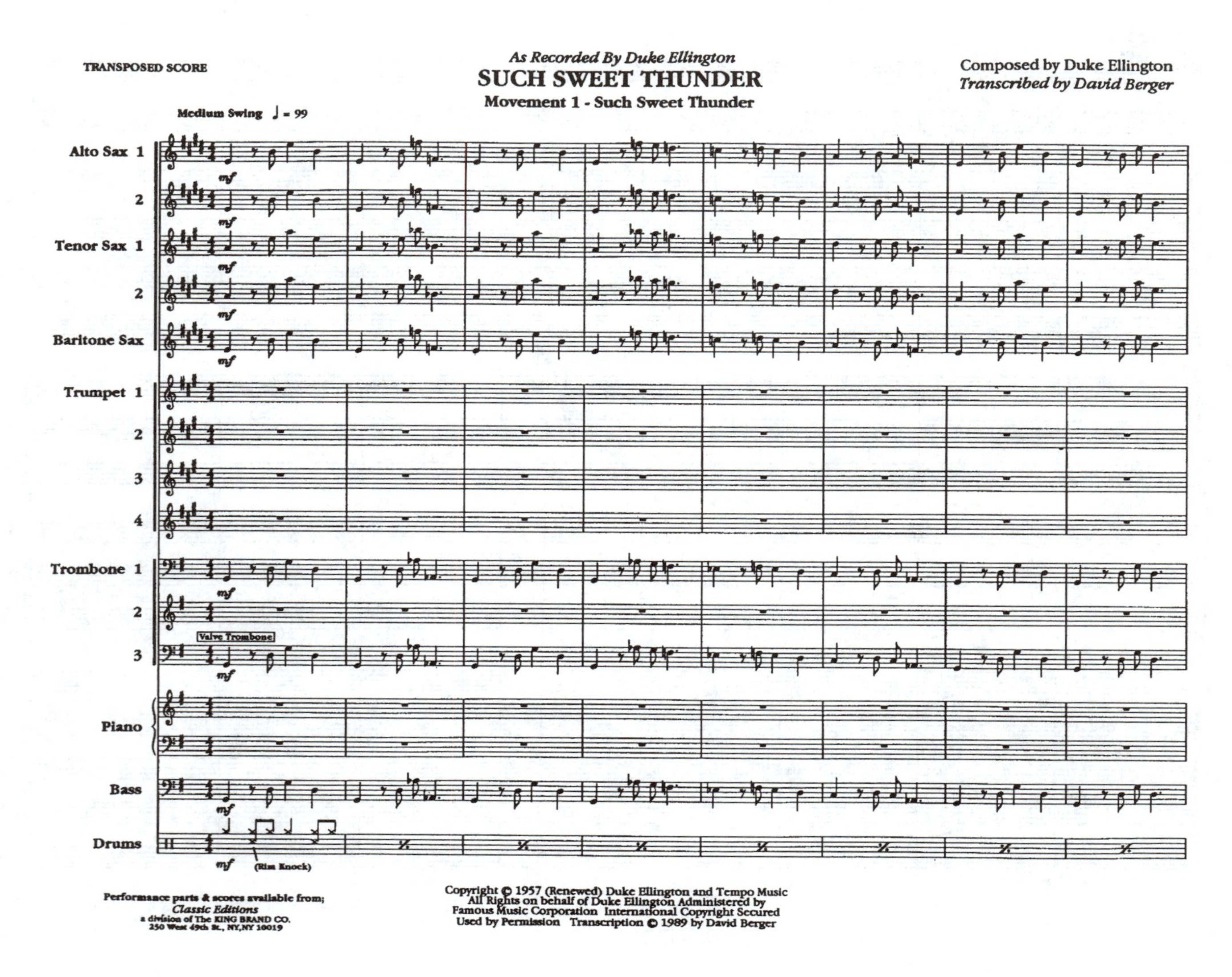
TRANSPOSED SCORE
As Recorded By Duke Ellington
SUCH SWEET THUNDER
Movement 1 - Such Sweet Thunder
Composed by Duke Ellington
Transcribed by David Berger
Medium Swing ♩ = 99
Alto Sax 1
2
Tenor Sax 1
2
Baritone Sax
Trumpet 1
2
3
4
Trombone 1
2
Valve Trombone
3
Piano
Bass
Drums
mf
(Rim Knock)
Performance parts & scores available from;
Classic Editions
a division of The KING BRAND CO.
250 West 49th St., NY,NY 10019
Copyright © 1957 (Renewed) Duke Ellington and Tempo Music
All Rights on behalf of Duke Ellington Administered by
Famous Music Corporation International Copyright Secured
Used by Permission Transcription © 1989 by David Berger

Alto 1
2
Tenor 1
2
Bari.
Trpt. 1
2
3
4
Tbn. 1
2
3
Pno.
Bs.
Dr.
Wa
15ma
8vabassa

A

Alto 1
2
Tenor 1
2
Bari.
Trpt. 1
2
3
4
Tbn. 1
2
3
Pno.
Bs.
Dr.

mf

Plunger w/mute

Wa Wa

f

15ma

3

Alto 1
2
Tenor 1
2
Bari.

Trpt. 1 — Wa Wa / Wa Wa Wa / Wa / Wa Wa Wa / Wa Wa / Wa Wa Wa / Wa Wa / Wa — To Open
2 — Wa Wa / Wa Wa Wa / Wa / Wa Wa Wa / Wa Wa / Wa Wa Wa / Wa Wa / Wa — To Open
3
4

Tbn. 1
2 — Wa Wa / Wa Wa Wa / Wa / Wa Wa Wa / Wa Wa / Wa Wa Wa / Wa Wa / Wa — To Open
3

Pno. — 15ma / 15ma / 15ma

Bs.

Dr.

B

Alto 1
2
Tenor 1
2
Bari.
Trpt. 1
2
3
4
Tbn. 1
2
3
Pno.
Bs.
Dr.

15ma

G D7 G G7 C7 G Bm7 B♭m7

3

SUCH SWEET THUNDER
5
C
Even 8ths
Alto 1
2
Tenor 1
2
Bari.
Trpt. 1
2
3
4
Tbn. 1
2
3
Pno.
Bs.
Dr.
Open - Solo
A7 D D♯o A A7
Am7 D7 G D7 G7 C C♯o G G7
mp
f

Alto 1
2
Tenor 1
2
Bari.
Trpt. 1
2
3
4
Tbn. 1
2
3
Pno.
Bs.
Dr.
mf
D7
D♯o
A
C♯m7
F♯7
Bm7
E7sus4
A
Open
C7
C♯o
G
Bm7
E7
Am7
D7
G
A♭

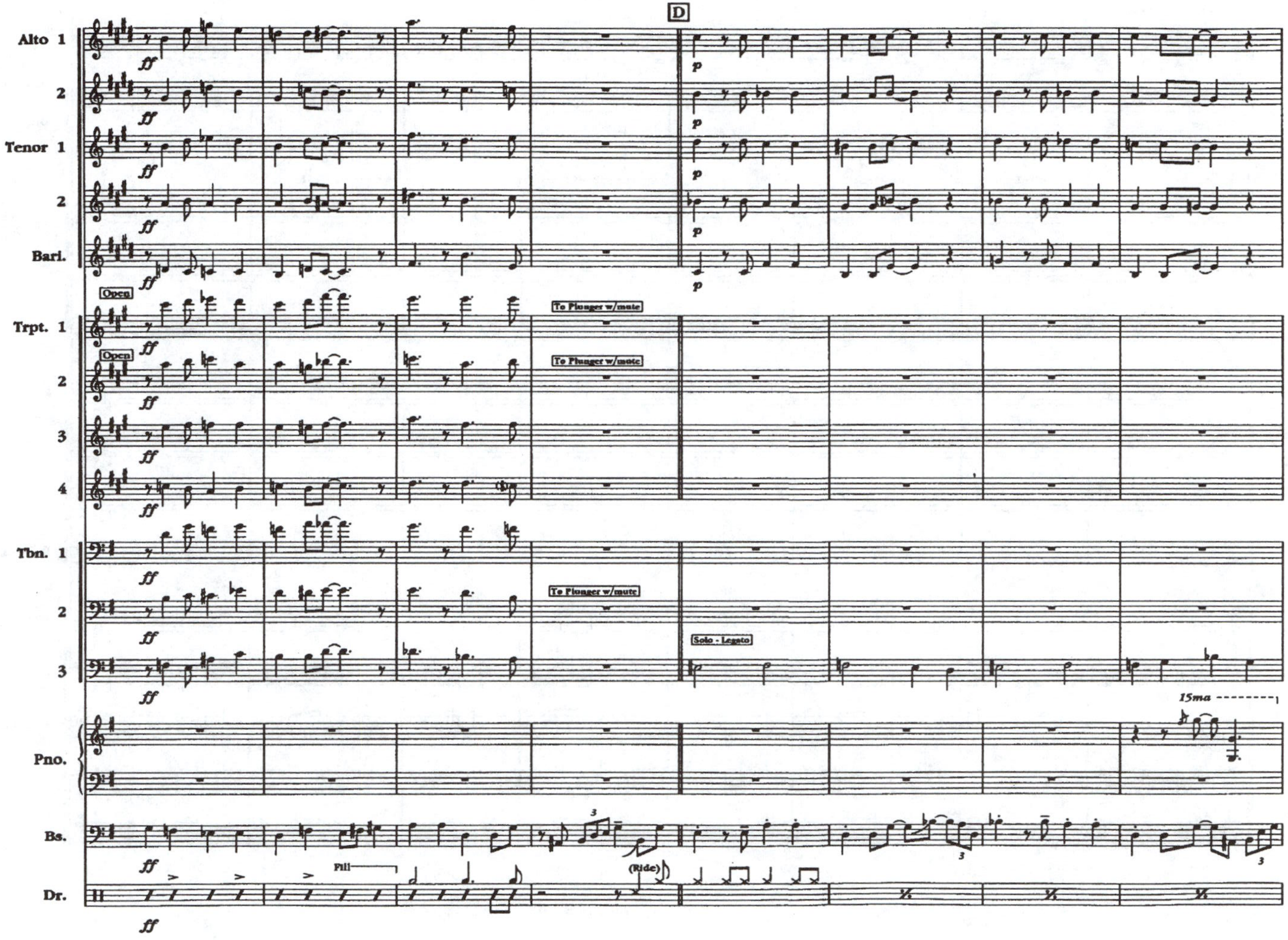
D
Alto 1
2
Tenor 1
2
Bari.
Trpt. 1
2
3
4
Tbn. 1
2
3
Pno.
Bs.
Dr.
ff
p
Open
Open
To Plunger w/mute
To Plunger w/mute
To Plunger w/mute
Solo - Legato
15ma
Fill
(Ride)
3

Alto 1
2
Tenor 1
2
Bari.
Trpt. 1
2
3
4
Tbn. 1
2
3
15ma
Pno.
Bs.
Dr.
(through the drums)

E
Alto 1
2
Tenor 1
2
Bari.
Trpt. 1
2
3
4
Tbn. 1
2
3
Pno.
Bs.
Dr.
Plunger w/mute
Plunger w/mute
Plunger w/mute
Wa Wa
15ma
mf
f

Clark Terry, special guest soloist with the Pittsburgh Jazz Orchestra.

The International Conference of the Duke Ellington Society, hosted by the Billy Strayhorn chapter of the society, held its 13th annual concert in Pittsburgh from May 24-28, 1995. The conference focused on the music of Duke Ellington and Billy Strayhorn and began with the grand opening concert featuring guest artists Clark Terry, Kenny Burrell, Louie Bellson and Jimmy Woode. The Pittsburgh Jazz Orchestra, a jazz repertoire orchestra directed by Nathan Davis, performed original compositions by both Ellington and Strayhorn. One of the highlights of the event was the premiere of a work entitled Blue House, a previously unreleased work edited by Walter van de Leur. Featured during the week-long program was a special duo concert featuring Geri Allen and McCoy Tyner. The following evening, the Dutch Jazz Orchestra, a jazz repertoire orchestra from Holland, performed a program which featured previously unpublished works directed by Jerry van Rooijen. The conference was well attended, attracting participants from 11 countries

Nathan Davis and the Pittsburgh Jazz Orchestra.

As further proof of Ellington's place in music history as a piano soloist, Rattenbury states:

> Ellington recalled one gladiatorial recital of improvised music involving all three men. Mexico's (a club in Harlem), was the scene of many battles of music in the late 1920's. Willie "The Lion" played there and it was a natural place for all piano players to hang out. I shall never forget the night Fats Waller, James P. Johnson and "The Lion" tangled there. Too bad there were no tape recorders in those days. (Rattenbury, p. 68)

Ellington's recollection of his performances at house rent parties in Harlem offers another indication of the fierce competition that existed among pianists during the 1920s. According to Ellington, he would often go to these various parties with some of the more established pianists (such as the legendary Lippy) in order to gain entrance (perhaps because he felt he did not measure up to the standards set by his colleagues, and therefore chose to go in the company of some of the more technically accomplished pianists). However, as Ellington's ability progressed and he became more skilled on the piano, he gained more confidence as a performer of his own works and of the compositions of others.

Rattenbury also quotes Ellington's reaction to the music of Jelly Roll Morton: "Morton played piano like one of those high school teachers in Washington. As a matter of fact, high school teachers played better jazz." (Rattenbury, p. 24) Whether or not Ellington disliked Jelly Roll Morton's highly technical approach to improvisation instead of Ellington's own laid back approach is debatable. I believe that Ellington, who had been raised in the elite metropolitan environment of Washington, D.C., in some ways resented Morton, a Creole who had literally appointed himself (to the dismay of many of his colleagues) as the creator of jazz and who had assumed the position as that music's most important spokesperson.

Regardless of the above discussion, historically, Jelly Roll Morton was an exceptional pianist. He accomplished feats like playing complicated ragtime pieces backwards, while at the same time utilizing various melodic embellishments and modulations—to the amazement of the original composers, who were often present in the audience. There is no doubt that Jelly Roll Morton was one of the great performers of all time.

Another aspect of Ellington's work that proved him superior to his contemporaries was his almost obsessive attention to sound and quality. According to John Edward Hasse in *Beyond Category: The Life and Genius of Duke Ellington:*

> If Ellington strove to achieve recordings of high musical quality, he also aimed at a high sonic quality. Drawing on his strengths as a listener, he worked to insure optimal balance of the instruments in relation to one another and, crucially, to the microphone that was just being introduced to recordmaking. (Hasse, p. 93)

Hasse's statement substantiates my earlier claim that Ellington imitated both the sophistication of the music of Western European symphonic orchestras as well as the music of dance bands of the northeastern U.S. In fact, one of the reasons Ellington and his orchestra sometimes found it difficult to tour through the Midwest, especially during the early years, was because the audience did not appreciate the sophisticated style of his music compared with the more rugged type of dance band music preferred in that (the Midwest) part of the country. The Midwestern bands appeared to be more interested in shaping rhythms than in perfecting the sounds of the music.

Ellington soon began to gear his music toward the recording studio instead of the many personal dance appearances to which he had been accustomed. In relation to this, Hasse states:

> Take any 1920s record by Fletcher Henderson and compare it with the contemporary Duke Ellington disc, and you will hear that Henderson didn't care about studio balances or (except on very rare occasions) tailor his recorded performances to best fit the time imposed by the 78 rpm format. Paul Whiteman was well ahead of Fletcher Henderson in this respect but even he lagged behind Ellington. *(Beyond Category)*

Again, we see that Ellington was interested in the overall sound of the music. Translated into a more philosophical approach to jazz, Ellington appeared to be more concerned with the way his music fit into society and how it was perceived by the listening public rather than how engaging or entertaining the music was for dancing. This illustrates again Ellington's preoccupation with sound over rhythm and dance.

Ellington was probably one of the greatest and earliest spokesmen for African Americans and their social issues, as evidenced by many of the titles of his compositions. In a quote from *Beyond Category* (Hasse), Ellington states, "Every one of my song titles is taken principally from the life of Harlem . . . I look to the everyday life and customs of the Negro to supply my inspiration." Titles such as *East Saint Louis Toodle-oo,* according to Ellington, reflected the particular way Negro laborers would walk after a hard day's work. Other compositions such as *Creole Love Call, Black and Tan Fantasie, The Moochie, Harlem River Quiver, Jungle Jamboree, Jungle Nights* and *Hottentot* (all created and performed during Ellington's stay at the Cotton Club in Harlem) represented the inspirations of African American life.

Ellington as a composer developed along the lines of a show band or theatrical composer, which might account for the sophistication of his orchestra. In 1927, during his prolonged engagement at the Cotton Club, Ellington gained his most important experience as a composer. In fact, according to Gunther Schuller in Hasse's *Beyond Category,* this period was one of Duke's most important because it provided him with a home base.

The importance of the Cotton Club engagement to Ellington's development as a composer cannot be overemphasized. It represented, as Gunther Schuller has written, a kind of prolonged workshop period, (Hasse, p. 1090) and it explains Ellington's involvement in both the performance and compositional aspects of music. At the Cotton Club, Ellington was able to use his band as a workshop for his compositions; he could hear his own music performed immediately after he composed it.

His band also developed considerably during the Cotton Club years. According to Andre Hodier and Gunther Schuller in Hasse's *Beyond Category,*

Ellington capitalized considerably on the solo talents of the members of his orchestra (especially trumpeter Bubber Miley and Tricky Sam Nanton) in developing his famous jungle sounds. In order to produce these sounds, the performer used hats and plungers to alter the natural sound of the instrument, imitating the natural sounds of lions, tigers, elephants and other animals in the jungle. These techniques were an important part of the show at the Cotton Club and helped to give the band a certain identity during the Harlem Renaissance.

JAZZ, An Original African American Art Form

Perhaps the most widely known musical contribution of African Americans in the world today is jazz, a style that has changed the face of music wherever it has been introduced. Its dynamic rhythms and compelling melodies have seduced the world and many of the world's most famous composers have stated that they changed their concept and approach to music after having heard African American jazz for the first time. To say that jazz is a popular music is to understate its importance and effect on world culture. If, in fact, jazz has played such an important role in changing the way humans relate to music, what then is this music we call jazz?

Jazz has been described by many of its practitioners as an improvised music based on the blues (a derivative of African church music and various forms of worksongs). In fact, jazz and blues are so similar that historians, in their research on the history of jazz, often overlook the earliest influences on both forms, and instead begin their studies with the music of New Orleans. To trace the true elements of jazz, researchers should start with its most seminal ingredients: African American worksongs and religious songs.

Jazz was born on plantations throughout North America, beginning with the interaction between Western Europeans and Western Africans. Early accounts of the association between jazz and religious music dates back to the mid-1700's. During the first half of the 1800's, African American religious music began to separate from non-religious music, and the division became permanent by the time jazz reached New Orleans. While it would be incorrect to say that jazz began in New Orleans, it did, however, find a home there. Although jazz havens existed throughout the south and in other areas of North America, New Orleans served as one of its first focal points in the history of jazz.

The music that emanated from New Orleans is referred to as "Dixieland," a term that is, at best, a misnomer. I once had the opportunity to interview the great banjoist/guitarist Danny Barker (author of *Bourbon Street Black: The New Orleans Black Jazzman,* New York: Oxford University Press, 1973) during his performance at the New Orleans club, Lou's and Charlie's on Rampart Street (Charlie Bryce, proprietor). To Barker and his colleagues, Dixieland had always been traditional New Orleans music, and during intermission, I listened to some of it playing on the jukebox. Bassist Julius Farmer, who had been appearing with me along with Ellis Marsalis, pointed out that the music on the jukebox was a traditional type of New Orleans music, somewhat resembling the music of the French Caribbean islands of Martinique and Guadeloupe, although the island music tends to have less blues in it. From a rhythmical point of view, however, and from the standpoint of feel, there appeared to be a great similarity between the two types of music, possibly because both Martinique and Guadeloupe are French-speaking and New Orleans, during the early stages of jazz, was a French possession.

Early in its history, the term jazz had not yet been used to describe the music played by African Americans; instead, music was identified by its geographical area. For example, visitors to New Orleans often used the term Dixieland to refer to the music played in the area where the French ten note piece (monetary script) was used. Music from the Northeast was referred to as Northeastern music; the Midwest as Midwestern music and the Southwest as Southwestern music. The music from New Orleans was from the "dix land" area because of its special relationship to France. The eventual mispronunciation of the French word "dix" led to the development of the term Dixieland, and because of its popular acceptance, the term Dixieland will be used in describing this style of music.

Because of its popularity, Dixieland became the music most of the world associates with the original jazz sound—and perhaps the most popular and greatest of the New Orleans Dixieland musicians was Louis Armstrong. Louis Armstrong (trumpeter/cornetist) is highly regarded as the very first serious soloist in jazz.

During the early periods of jazz, most musicians tended to improvise from or "jazz up" the melody (a march, waltz or folk song). The artist would begin his presentation by playing a loose or "ragged" version of the melody. After stating this "ragged" version of the melody, the artist would then improvise on this melody, creating variations which became more intense with the repetition of each chorus.

The significance of early New Orleans jazz music was in its use of collective improvisation, which occurred when the musicians performed together not only the melody but also the improvisation. This is in sharp contrast with the styles of the later years, especially Chicago jazz, New York jazz and Swing, where the soloist stood alone, functioning as a featured artist above the band background. The idea of collective improvisation, without placing emphasis on a particular soloist, reemerged during the 1960s. Archie Shepp, Albert Ayler and Marion Brown would often say they were playing the original music because they were following the same concept of collective improvisation that the originators of jazz also utilized.

In their research, musical historians have focused primarily on the jazz period in New Orleans, followed closely by the music of Ragtime, centered in the Midwest around places like Sedalia, St. Joseph and Joplin, Missouri. It was in the Midwest that salesmen, tourists and other travelers across the United States found refuge, and the need to entertain these travelers was the impetus which gave birth to numerous clubs and piano bars. These piano bars soon became the home of the most innovative Ragtime musicians, particularly Scott Joplin, perhaps one of the most popular and important figures of this era who later became known as the "Father of Ragtime."

Ragtime was first considered a non-jazz form. There were numerous articles written about it as a separate music, independent of jazz, an assessment probably due to its "ragged" or loose style of playing.

Ragtime initially was a guitar music, developed in the Midwest wherever there were itinerant mining camps. Many of the mining camps set up small, one-room (shot-gun) taverns or bars that featured a lone blues/ragtime guitar player. As soon as the area had been strip-mined completely, the mining company would tear down the temporary tavern and move on to another site. Because these sites only lasted as long as the area was being mined, it was important to be able to pick up and move fast; thus, the need for entertainment that could relocate easily. The blues/ragtime guitar player would pick up his instrument and be on his way to the next location.

Many of these early ragtime guitar players were also singers. They played a "shuffle" style that later became synonymous with not only ragtime but also boogie-woogie. Any relationship that may have existed between jazz and ragtime was eliminated because of the perception of ragtime by jazz musicians and fans who did not associate rag with jazz because it borrowed the music and styles of classical composition.

As Ragtime moved south towards New Orleans, the classical connotations were dismissed and Ragtime was accepted as jazz music. Many of the piano players in and around the Sedalia, Missouri area had been trained as classical musicians; their style and sound possessed many elements of classical music. The Ragtime style of music was distinguished by its geographical area and time period. The early era was centered primarily around three Missouri locations: Sedalia, St. Joseph and Joplin, where the music was predominantly classical in nature.

As Ragtime progressed stylistically and geographically, it began to transform and take on other characteristics. For example, when Ragtime moved into the St. Louis, Missouri area, it became more "show like" and danceable, and used much more syncopation in its rhythms. Finally Ragtime moved to New Orleans where its stylistic character was based more on the "blues."

Many early historians have stated that Ragtime started during the middle 1800s; these same historians have said that Dixieland music originated in the late 1800s and early 1900s. According to this information, Ragtime would be older than Dixieland, which is not the case. The fact is Ragtime and Dixieland existed during the same time periods, but flourished in different parts of the country.

Many scholars identify the 1920s as the most important era of the blues. Perhaps this is true from the standpoint of an organized musical form, having twelve bars; but blues, in fact, is more than a form. It is a feeling—a concept. A sensual yet philosophical approach to life and its problems. The blues always has been an intricate and vital part of the African American existence in the United States, and dates back to the plantation, where the work song, field holler and street cry originated.

During the early years of the blues (before it had been assigned a form by historians) , it was thought that every individual could sing the blues, able to express his or her problems and/or successes in song. Another misconception about the blues is that it is a sad music. The blues also exists in the form of religious blues, work blues and folk blues. The type of situation or "feeling" of the performer along with the story they wish to tell dictates the sentiment expressed in the blues performed. Therefore, the blues could be happy or sad, bright or dark, elated or melancholy, but all resting in the hands, heart and voice (or instrument) of the performer. Most jazz musicians, whether they play modern jazz, mainstream, bebop, swing or ragtime, all rely heavily on the blues when improvising. In Paris, I remember once asking veteran saxophonist Johnny Griffin to share with me some of his "secrets" on improvisation. Griffin told me: "Nathan, no matter what you play, be sure you play the blues in it. If it's a religious song, play some blues in it, if it's a show tune . . . play some blues in it." According to Griffin, that was the mark of a true jazz musician.

The blues is and has always been the basis of jazz. However, the irony of the blues today is that blues musicians are distinguished as separate from jazz musicians when, in fact, they are one and the same. The way this separation came about is very disturbing. During the 1940s, many jazz musicians actually earned their living playing the blues, most notably, Charlie Parker. His early recordings with the Jay McShann Band find Parker playing the blues. I was astounded then to learn that most musicians who were trained in music schools were under the impression that Charlie Parker always played bebop, when, in fact, he played the "chicken shack" circuit—as did B.B. King and other blues musicians.

The distinction between jazz and blues—"the line of musical separation"—was created by the music industry (record company producers, publishers, promoters, etc.), in order to insure a particular market for each product, i.e., blues and jazz. This separation is unfortunate for young musicians coming up because as a result of this separation they tend to look down on blues musicians, the forefathers of jazz. Instead, young musicians believe they are better musicians because they play a different music called jazz. To correct this problem, all musicians should be introduced at an early stage during the educational process to the importance of the blues.

Another form of jazz was the big band era or the jazz age that took place during the 1920s in Chicago and New York. The early big bands were "little big bands" that consisted of a traditional number of saxophones and brass. Where normally a big band used five saxophones, four trumpets and four trombones, the little big bands used three saxophones and three or four combined brass players.

The closing of the Port of New Orleans in 1917, due to the killing of a sailor during a knife fight in the Storyville section of the city, was the primary reason for the movement of jazz to Chicago and later New York. The killing had prompted the Department of Defense to place the entire Storyville area off-limits to military personnel. This action, as well as the pickets and boycotts by feminists and special interest groups, forced many Storyville business owners to close their doors on this "sinful" yet lively and historic part of New Orleans.

According to the Bureau of Vital Statistics, the largest migration of blacks from the rural south to the urban areas of the northeast occurred between 1910 and 1920. Musicians followed these migrations in order to continue working. In Chicago, the more sophisticated high society audiences found their music styles too rough and unsophisticated, so these musical migrants were forced to restructure their music in order to accommodate the dance crowds of the 1920s.

One example is Joe Oliver, who left New Orleans and became quite successful in Chicago. According to historians, Oliver had watered down his music so it would be accepted by Chicago audiences. But to keep things hopping, he sent for Louis Armstrong, whom he featured occasionally as a "hot" soloist.

Many different musical styles existed simultaneously in Chicago during the third post-migration era. As a result of this early migration of southern jazz and blues artists, Chicago eventually became a haven for jazz and blues. Eventually, there was the urban blues of Bo Diddley, Muddy Waters, Willie Dixon, Howlin Wolf and Memphis Slim. However these artists and styles were preceded by the Chicago Boogie-Woogie school, headed by Albert Ammons. Other artists of this period included Clarence "Pinetop" Smith, Meade "Lux" Lewis, and Pete Johnson. On the north side of Chicago were society dance bands that were being imitated on the south side by black bands headed by King Joe Oliver and others.

During this same period, the Harlem Renaissance was in full bloom in New York. The Harlem Renaissance—a period that focused on the art, music, history and culture of African Americans—was a showcase era for the African American in the U.S., demonstrating the development from slave to primary contributor in American society.

During the Harlem renaissance of the 1920's, black businesses sprang up in Harlem as African American entrepreneurs began to buy back valuable property previously owned by whites. Large dance bands formed, artistic and social clubs developed, literary artists began to write black plays, record and movie companies and distribution houses were created (e.g., Black Swan Records) to meet the needs of African American cultural development. This cultural activity, combined with the introduction of the talking pictures and the distribution of recordings of African American artists, created a boom for African American music.

The Harlem big bands, considered by many to be the most important contribution of this era, were the stepping stones for one of America's greatest composers, Duke Ellington. Other Harlem big bands were led by Elmer Snowden, Chick Webb, William McKinney (William McKinney and The McKinney Cottonpickers), Luis Russell, Sam Woodings, and later, Don Redman.

Another important development of the Renaissance period was the Harlem Piano school. Piano players such as Thomas "Fats" Waller, James P. Johnson and Willie "The Lion" Smith proved to be comparable in technical abilities to their classical counterparts yet were able to forge a new direction in the area of jazz piano.

One of the primary and most distinct players of this Harlem piano school was Art Tatum. Although Tatum arrived on the scene much later than the aforementioned pianists, he is often referred to as the "Dean" of this school. Although Tatum, who hailed from Toledo, Ohio, was blind, he was able to thoroughly integrate various styles of classical and jazz music into his phenomenal improvisations, which set him apart from other artists of his generation.

8 The Music of Thelonius Monk and John Coltrane

John Coltrane

John Coltrane has been credited with pushing the boundaries of the tenor and soprano saxophones in jazz and, in some instances, music to the very limits of acceptability. During the mid-1960s—considered by many to have been his most musically aggressive period—his often robust, aggressive flirtation with the then avant-garde left many of his previously devoted fans in a confused state of musical anarchy. Yet the stereotype of the angry, militant, black jazz musician did not seem to apply to John, who was one of the most gentle men I have ever had the pleasure of meeting. Occasionally crouching over his saxophone as if he were in some kind of meditative trance, Coltrane would create some of the most innovative and unconventional sounds conceivable. Just who was John Coltrane and why did he risk everything he had worked so hard to accomplish by flirting with the avant-garde during the 1960s?

John Coltrane was born September 23, 1926 in Hamlet, North Carolina, and died on July 17, 1967. According to jazz historian and Coltrane scholar Bill Cole (*John Coltrane,* Schirmer books), Coltrane was exposed to music at an early age. His grandfather, a southern Methodist minister, was responsible for exposing him to Afro American religious music. His father J.R. (John Robert) Coltrane, who played guitar, sang and played several other music instruments, and his mother, who played piano (J.C. Thomas, *Chasin the Trane,* Doubleday), were directly responsible for influencing young John's musical taste. Perhaps it was his strong exposure to African American religious music that gave young Coltrane his soulful and highly spiritual approach to jazz, an approach that can be seen in later works such as *A Love Supreme, Spiritual, Manifestation and Lord Help Me to Be.* (*The Encyclopedia of Jazz in the 70s,* Leonard Feather) A close examination of A Love Supreme provides an insight into Coltrane's spiritual approach to jazz.

To understand any form of music—jazz, classical, folk, etc.—it is important to grasp its spiritual and philosophical elements. In this regard, ethnomusicologists have done a considerable amount of work in bringing this aspect of music scholarship to the forefront, but not until the 1980s, in the case

Thelonius Monk. Archive Photos/Frank Driggs Collection.

of jazz, blues and other forms of African American music, have they adequately focused on this question of spirituality and philosophy in music. Notes and chord sequences do not make the music; it is the spiritual content of the music that gives it its essence. Combined with the intellect and the sensitivity of the music maker and the listener, a series of notes and chords take on a life of their own and eventually become music.

Critics often compare Coltrane's linear approach to improvisation to that of the great tenor saxophonist, Dexter Gordon. While Coltrane's style during the early years did have a lot in common with the laid back rhythmic approach often associated with Dexter Gordon's style, Coltrane's sound and phrasing was more closely allied to the style of tenor saxophonist, Sonny Stitt.

A close examination of Dexter Gordon's work shows that his phrases tend to be more rhythmic than either Coltrane's or Stitt's. Gordon's phrases also tend to be much shorter. Examples of these differences are found in the following phrase which simulates Dexter's style.

The phrase, at this point, is a two bar phrase which starts on Eb (the minor 3rd of a C7 chord) and ends on a Bb (the minor 7th of the same chord). Although Dexter Gordon was often associated with short "memorable" musical quotes, he, on occasion would insert long beautifully constructed lines.

In example R.A.-III, we find a typical Dexter Gordon phrase that consists of a fluid four (4) measures and is primarily linear rather than the typical rhythmic phrases commonly used by Dexter.

John Coltrane. Archive Photos/Frank Driggs Collection.

The beginning of the phrase starts with an Eb eighth note pickup which is used as a launching point for the ever popular triplet figure which was one of the rhythmical pillars of the bebop era. The line then proceeds to a semi chromatic descent (here I use the term semi to illustrate that the phrase does not, in this particular case, utilize a pure chromatic line but, instead, is altered to

All musical examples are original composed ideas by Nathan Davis and are intended to simulate the work of the artist.

R.A. II In the style of Dexter Gordon

Med. Swing

Computerized music examples by
Mary Ann Morroco

ensure a more unified approach). Beginning on C, the line descends down the chromatic scale, briefly interrupting the continuity by omitting the Ab and proceeding directly to the G. Thus, we find that the first group of four (4) notes set up a kind of jazz tetrachord which is then continued a step lower. The

R.A. III In the style of Dexter Gordon

second group of notes begin on G followed by F#, F then moves up to a high C (a skip of a fifth), represents again what I referred to earlier as a semi-tetrachord.

By jumping from the F (which appears on the 4th beat of the 1st measure), the phrase creates a different color by utilizing the already familiar chromaticism. The above phrases are typical of the work of John Coltrane during his early years and of Sonny Stitt throughout his career.

Example R.A.-IV is a typical Sonny Stitt phrase which also utilized the eighth note as a launching note for the popular triplet figure, which is then followed by the four note jazz tetrachord. However, as one can clearly see in

R.A. IV In the style of Sonny Stitt

Computerized music examples by
Mary Ann Morroco

this particular case, as is more typical in Stitt's work, he favors the use of the diatonic or whole tone scale grouping over the chromatic scales often associated with the work of Dexter Gordon.

Example R.A.-V is a typical Coltrane phrase that also utilizes the eighth-note pickup to the triplet figure which sets the stage for the use of the descending chordal figure. (Again, we see the use of the jazz tetrachord figure but, this time it takes the form of a Bbm7 chord played in reverse.) The high point of this phrase occurs on the high Bb on the 1st beat of the second measure. This phrase is the type of melodic motive that permeates the work of all three saxophonists: Dexter Gordon, Sonny Stitt and John Coltrane. However, I have found

R.A. V In the style of John Coltrane

Computerized music examples by
Mary Ann Morroco

that Coltrane's earlier periods beginning with his work with the band of Earl Bostic show that his work tends to reflect some of Gordon's style but, is more influenced by the style of Sonny Stitt as opposed to Gordon.

The first time I had the opportunity to hear John Coltrane was in 1954. I was a high school student in my home town of Kansas City and Coltrane was in town performing at a dance with the Earl Bostic band. During this time, my fellow students and I were mastering transcribed solos of major jazz saxophonists like Coleman Hawkins, Sonny Rollins, Sonny Stitt and Charlie Parker. What is ironic is that none of us had studied music theory. Regardless, we discovered that Coltrane's style was closely allied to that of saxophonist Sonny Stitt, especially Stitt's more linear, scale-like approach on tenor saxophone.

It was not until much later that I began to read (with some amusement) that critics equated Coltrane's style to Dexter Gordon's more laid back rhythmic approach. Although Dexter's approach to phrasing seemed to incorporate the best of tenor saxophonists Lester Young, Coleman Hawkins and Don Byas, I could find little or no evidence supporting the claim that Coltrane had been heavily influenced by Dexter's style. Although Dexter Gordon was definitely one of our musical heroes, it was Sonny Stitt who Trane most imitated.

For the student of African American music, especially jazz, one of the most interesting aspects of Coltrane's music is his use of a variety of styles. Coltrane, more than any other jazz musician, perhaps with the exception of Miles Davis, was able to change styles at will, without sacrificing any of his musical integrity.

Miles Davis, as well as Charlie Parker, was responsible for the introduction of some of the most subdued lyrical lines during the bebop period. During the early 1950s, Davis used a softer, more lyrical approach that eventually gave birth to the "Cool" style of playing. Many critics described the sound as resembling "a chicken walking on crushed egg shells." During the latter half of the 1950s, Davis, in a more aggressive, soulful role, became one of the emerging leaders of what was known as mainstream or hard bop. Around 1959, Miles emerged as the leader of what some historians like to call the modal jazz period. During this period, Miles and his colleagues, including John Coltrane, began to experiment with substituting modes for chord changes, thus giving the soloist more freedom. In the early 1960s, Miles progressed toward a freer style which became known as the avant-garde, but it was not until he made the recording of ESP that many of his colleagues began to listen seriously to some of the more daring styles of the younger avant-garde players of that period. Again, it was Miles Davis who provided a "musical legitimacy" to what was then called "Jazz-Rock" and later "Jazz-Fusion." However, given the often harsh treatment Coltrane received from the critics during his so-called avant-garde period, I am sure that there are those who would disagree with this assessment.

John Coltrane's musical virtuosity has influenced many saxophonists, including Pharaoh Saunders, Archie Shepp, Charles Lloyd, Michael Brecker, Wayne Shorter and Joe Henderson, and just about every other serious tenor saxophone player during the early 1960s.

The composition *T. for T.* (Time for Trane) composed in 1967 in Paris, France and originally published by Ursula Davis Musik-Verlag of Berlin, Germany (GEMA), is an example of the kind of influence John Coltrane had on the younger jazz musicians of the period. *T. for T.* was originally recorded for Sonnet Records in Stockholm, Sweden during the summer of 1969, with Leroy Lowe (drums), Red Mitchell (bass), Joe Sample (piano) and myself on tenor saxophone. This composition presents a kind of "double Coltrane challenge" for the improvising musician. Due to Coltrane's almost "God-like" technical ability to maneuver through the fast moving set of chord changes (changing every 2 beats), horn players, especially young saxophonists, felt a need to be able to play in and out of fast moving changes as did Trane. The way I approached learning to do this task was to compose tunes in a similar style. (Charlie "Bird" Parker and Dizzy Gillespie were masters of this technique in the 1940s.)

T. for T. (Time for Trane) begins on an F7 (for 2 beats) and then progresses to an Ab7 (for 2 beats) a minor 3rd away and finally comes to rest on a B7 (4 beats), which is an augmented fourth or minor fifth from the tonic of F7. This harmonic movement not only produces the now famous minor 3rd sequences put forth by Coltrane on Giant Steps, but also introduces an interesting series of melodic sequences based on the interval of the augmented 5th and perfect 4th and finally cumulating with a descending whole tone scale. The whole tone scale starts on Ab (lst beat of the 1st ending) and proceeds down the scale to D.

The B section, or bridge as it is often referred to, is introduced by a modulation up 1/2 step from the Db chord which is the first chord of the second ending to the Dm7, G7 which then becomes the IIm7 / V7 of the new key of C. The bridge continues to alternate between the Dm7/G7 (IIm7 V7) chord in measures one, two and three. The Gm7 C7 is then used as a pivot in measure 4, modulating to (IIm7 V7) the key of F for one measure in measure 5. Beginning in measure six with the Eb7, the harmonic progression descends using a whole

R.A. VI

T. for T.

Composed by
Nathan Davis
Paris France
1967
aug. 5th
whole tone scale
Bridge

tone sequence until the D in measure eight. What is also unusual about this pattern is that the 6th remains in the melody of each chord, thus introducing yet another dimension to the challenge of the Coltranian sequential improvisational style.

But who were the artists who influenced and inspired Coltrane? Although I am certain the list includes Charlie Parker, Lester Young, Coleman Hawkins, Dexter Gordon and, according to Coltrane himself, alto saxophonist Johnny Hodges, careful examination of Coltrane's solo transcriptions of the late 1950s and early 1960s reveals that his most important musical influence was as I have previously stated, saxophonist Sonny Stitt. At the time John Coltrane first surfaced on the national scene, Sonny Stitt was already a well-established recording artist. Sonny, who originally played alto saxophone, decided to switch to tenor sax after hearing "Bird", Charlie Parker. In fact, saxophonists like Sonny Stitt, John Coltrane, Jimmy Heath and Johnny Griffin were in awe of Charlie Parker. They also felt, to some degree, that Parker's virtuosity on the instrument left little to be desired. Whether or not these musicians were actually intimidated by Parker's virtuoso playing on the alto is debatable; history has proven that the above mentioned players were indeed virtuoso players themselves. However, the fact still remains that Parker literally had the field of jazz alto saxophone playing to himself.

Whereas Stitt had concentrated originally on the alto, he began to assert himself on the recently acquired tenor and then proceeded to record a couple of sides on baritone saxophone, that today stands as a landmark for jazz recordings on that instrument.

Sonny's influence on the baritone, although not widely publicized, was immense. His tone on the baritone was big and aggressive and he played with the same agility and fluency on the larger instrument that he had displayed on the much lighter sounding alto and tenor saxophones. Although Sonny's linear approach to improvising most influenced John Coltrane, critics who linked the sound of tenor saxophonist Dexter Gordon to that of John Coltrane were correct in pointing out the similarities in their sound. However, as I have previously pointed out, the manner in which both artists approached the linear concept of improvisation suggests a closer link between the lighter, smooth approach of Sonny Stitt and Coltrane than existed between Gordon and Coltrane.

Coltrane's harmonic concept was probably greatly influenced by both Eddie "Clean Head" Vinson, Dizzy Gillespie, Miles Davis and Thelonius Monk. Because of the enormous amount of press given to the collaboration between Monk and Coltrane and his highly publicized recordings with Miles Davis' sextet, most jazz fans and historians readily acknowledge Coltrane's indebtedness to these artists. However, his musical allegiance to "Clean Head" Vinson is not readily recognized. Perhaps one of the reasons for this oversight is that, in the eyes of many critics, "Clean Head" was merely a blues or rhythm and blues artist rather than a jazz musician.

It is unfortunate that Eddie "Clean Head" Vinson is considered primarily a blues musician, and not an important contributor to jazz. According to saxophonist and jazz innovator Jimmy Heath, Vinson has been responsible for penning such jazz classics as *Tune Up and Four.* Jimmy also stated that during the

1940s, Eddie "Clean Head" Vinson became one of the most popular features in the big band of trumpeter Cootie Williams. Vinson was a musician who embodied the highest standards possible in African American music, as both a jazz and blues artist.

Coltrane probably acquired his approach to improvising from Charlie Parker. Parker would take standard compositions and literally make them his own—changing the melody completely while at the same time maintaining the basic harmonic scheme of the piece. This technique served two purposes: it provided Parker and his colleagues with an opportunity to improvise from a well known standard and at the same time it offered the musicians a chance to compose an original melody. The fact that the altered melody was legally considered an original melodic line gave Parker and his colleagues the right to collect royalties on an original work.

Many explanations have been given as to why Coltrane developed what became known as "sheets of sound." Basically, Trane practiced reading vertically-arranged arpeggios that usually were reserved for harpists. According to most of his colleagues, Coltrane practiced harp music and from piano instruction books to increase his speed in playing chords. He also used Nicholas Slonimsky's *Thesaurus of Scales and Melodic Patterns.* Consistent practice (he often practiced 6–7 hours daily) of this material gave him a tremendous amount of technique, speed and clarity. In fact the notes would go by so fast that anyone who heard them referred to his fast flurry of notes as "sheets of sound."

During various periods of his life, Coltrane literally was obsessed with sound.

> "I can remember going by Frank Wells' place in Chicago (Wells was a very popular Chicago-based mouth piece refacer/repairman) to have my mouth piece refaced in order to achieve a brighter and more clear sound. Wells immediately recalled an incident where Coltrane visited him while performing in Chicago. Coltrane came by with literally a pillow case full of mouth pieces and asked Wells to reshape (or reface) each of them. According to Wells, he had never seen a saxophonist with so many different mouth pieces to be refaced."

As a result of his earlier experience playing alto saxophone, his concept of sound on tenor resembled that of the higher sounding alto; it was more pointed and with a lighter edge. This concept in sound was then augmented by his attempt to duplicate the smoother silky sound of Johnny Hodges on alto. Most musicians and critics agree that Johnny Hodges possessed one of the most hauntingly beautiful sounds ever produced on the alto saxophone.

After switching from the alto to tenor saxophone, Coltrane attempted to find a pure, comparable tenor sound. Coltrane's sound on tenor, especially during the 1960s, had a penetrating, almost haunting effect, quite different from the sounds of the other prominent tenors like Sonny Rollins, and earlier, Gene Ammons. These tenor sax players produced a sound that was deep, heavy and robust. Coltrane and Sonny Stitt used a similar approach to sound because they both originally played alto and incorporated that sound into their music once they began to concentrate on the larger tenor saxophones.

Historically, the same can be said of tenor saxophonist Lester "Prez" Young. Most historians attribute "Prez's" light, airy and cool sound to the influences of saxophonist Frankie Traumbauer; Traumbauer, however, played a smaller C melody saxophone that produced a lighter sound by virtue of its size. Lester Young was also a very fine clarinetist and actually recorded on the instrument. During a visit to Tulane University's jazz archives in New Orleans (directed by curator and founder Dick Allen), I heard recordings of Prez playing solo clarinet as well as his customary tenor sax. In many ways, the sound played in the lower and middle registers of the clarinet by Jimmy Guiffre is reminiscent of Prez's sound on the same instrument. To determine the origins of a particular influence, especially when it comes to sound, the size, type, and shape of the instrument (especially the curve or straight soprano saxophone, as well as the cornet or trumpet) must be considered.

Coltrane's flirtation with the avant-garde was interesting and provocative. In many ways, it is difficult to discuss the avant-garde in terms of African American musicians because the avant-garde movement in jazz during the 1960s was so closely aligned with the black revolution that took place during the same period. It also would be inappropriate in this work to conduct a thorough investigation in the affect Trane had on his colleagues. Coltrane, however, was as much influenced by these factors as he was by the music of artists such as Eric Dolphy, Archie Shepp, Albert Ayler and, to some degree, Ornette Coleman.

It is important to mention the work of avant-garde saxophonist Albert Ayler in relation to John Coltrane's work. As John Coltrane became involved with the avant-garde, he found the work of Ayler more and more intriguing. When asked what saxophonist he would most like to emulate, Coltrane humbly replied that he would most like to play like Albert Ayler.

Albert Ayler was probably the most controversial and dynamic young tenor saxophonist of the avant-garde period; other performers included Archie Shepp, Guiseppi Logan and Frank Wright. Albert Ayler actually began as a rhythm and blues player. Many musicians at the time doubted whether Ayler really had the same experience as his colleagues in playing not only chord changes but also more structured types of music. Regardless of these apprehensions, historians agree that Ayler's music did make an impact and that he represented the sound of the avant-garde of the 1960s.

Critics, at least those who supported the work of Albert Ayler, were pleased to hear John Coltrane's remark and they went on to make quite a big deal out of the fact that Coltrane even had noticed the work of such a staunch avant-gardist. Armed with a glowing endorsement from one of the jazz world's most recognized performers, John Coltrane, the avant-garde performers found themselves in a very respected and greatly sought after position, i.e., recognized as legitimate.

Needless to say, Coltrane's endorsement of Ayler alienated some musicians and confused others. Perhaps Coltrane's intense interest in Ayler's work is due to his desire to stay in the forefront of the young avant-garde movement of the period; it is also possible that he simply found Ayler's work intellectually stimulating and challenging.

As a participant and observer of the jazz scene during this same period (1960s), I am positive that Coltrane appreciated Ayler's ability to improvise in an uninhibited manner and the freedom Ayler had to pursue whatever musical direction he wanted without the restriction of traditional theoretical rules. At heart, Coltrane was a disciple of freedom and, in fact, the concept of freedom is at the very basis of jazz.

From its very beginnings during the 1800s, the freedom to play what one felt as an expression of innermost feelings was at the heart of jazz improvisation. But while the true essence of jazz is embodied in the concept of freedom, the necessary theoretical guidelines that insure a true and pure performance can not be eliminated. What is in question here is how one actually approach this freedom, i.e., what are the methods used to obtain it? Should freedom be acquired through delicate study and careful examination of theoretical forms and the unquestionable mastery of a particular instrument, or should it be obtained by ignoring all the rules and boldly forging ahead with reckless abandonment?

In pondering these and similar questions concerning the avant-garde, a musical/socio-political division emerged between the avant-garde and the traditionalist. Traditionalists questioned whether Ayler and his colleagues learned jazz through a traditional theoretical approach to harmony, form and structure, eventually eliminating the rules once they were mastered. Or did they truly represent a new and innovative approach to playing jazz—a method free of the traditional theoretical rules?

Further evidence of Coltrane's involvement and continued interest in the avant-garde centered around his recording "Ascension." I remember being asked by several critics for my opinion on what I thought Coltrane was trying to accomplish on this recording. At the time the recording was released, I had been living and working with drummer Kenny Clarke at the Blue Note in Paris, and was deeply involved in the European jazz scene. It was only natural that the critics would seek me out, along with Woody Shaw, Larry Young and Billy Brooks, and several other younger players, for our opinions on certain new releases.

It was during this period that French producer Yves Chamberlain, the owner of Studio Davou in Paris, proposed that I make a recording with Coltrane's rhythm section. Although I was excited about the possibility of recording with such an important group, I suggested to Yves that he find someone else. I felt that I was not ready to make such a record at that time and I wanted to continue my work with Kenny Clarke and to study more theory. Yves refused and the date was scheduled.

Initially, Coltrane had given his approval for the date, but for business reasons, he objected to the idea of us using his entire rhythm section. Finally, French organist Eddie Louiss was added as a replacement for McCoy Tyner. The final date included Elvin Jones, drums; Jimmy Garrison, bass; Eddie Louiss, organ and piano; and myself, on tenor saxophone. After the session was concluded, Elvin Jones asked me if I would like to join Trane on the remainder of the tour because, as Elvin put it, Trane was beginning to include a lot of young musicians in his work. Because of my tremendous respect for Coltrane's work (Coltrane was like an icon for me and for many of my age group), I explained that I would like to remain in Paris until I felt ready to work with such a musical legend.

Approximately one year later Ascension was released, featuring a number of young musicians whom Coltrane had asked to join him in his improvisational experiment. After a careful examination of the recording, I concluded that Coltrane had indeed accomplished his initial goal of bringing together the natural, uninhibited sounds of the avant-garde with the more traditional sounds of jazz. But I still felt that the established musicians should have played a more significant role. I must admit that I also felt that some of the musicians on the recording were not as technically accomplished, and were more experimental, than others and therefore lacked the theoretical and technical capability to enhance the recording. Needless to say, this recording caused a flurry of controversy among musicians and critics. Was it music? Did all of the musicians involved really know what they were doing? These and many similar questions concerning this recording were never really answered, and the question of validity in jazz during the 1960s avant-garde period still remains, even today.

I am convinced that as Coltrane's flirtation with the avant-garde progressed, he began to think that spirituality, although an important aspect of music, must also be accompanied by the same degree of technical and theoretical knowledge and training. A careful examination of Ascension supports the idea that a musical division exists between musicians who are technically trained and those who lack such training.

One of Coltrane's most lyrical recordings was his ballads LP. (John Coltrane with Johnny Hartman: Impulse 40- March 6–7, 1963: Coltrane-tenor sax; McCoy Tyner-piano; Jimmy Garrison-bass; Elvin Jones-drums; Johnny Hartman-vocal; *They Say It's Wonderful; Lush Life; My Own and Only Love; Autumn Serenade; Dedicated to You; You Are Too Beautiful*) Here we find Coltrane at his best as he skillfully interpreted some of the most respected standards of our time.

Most critics considered Coltrane to be one of the most lyrical modern saxophonists of his time. This lyricism was acquired by listening to and imitating the styles of tenor saxophonist, Lester Young and alto saxophonist, Charlie Parker. One of the problems with the numerous imitators of Coltrane's lyrical approach to improvisation is that they do not realize the lyricism is linked to Parker. If imitators are going to understand and duplicate Trane's style, they should study Parker's work first.

At the risk of sounding like a close-minded devotee of bebop, I must admit that the music of Charlie Parker and his colleagues permeated the music of just about every jazz musician that followed them. Throughout the history of jazz, musicians have labeled their music under various names in order to gain a wider audience; many of them infused ethnic music from the Balkans, Latin America, North Africa and the East Indies. As an ethnomusicologist, my colleagues and I appreciate the inclusion of various ethnic music in jazz; but I am also concerned when the inclusion of various ethnic music in jazz omits its most important ethnic music—the basis and foundation of jazz—the blues.

Once the music enters into the realm of jazz, the presence of blues cannot be denied. Parker and his colleagues honored this theory and that is one of the reasons that their music, bebop, has stood the test of time and remains a vital force in jazz today.

Another important factor in jazz is the volume of recordings Coltrane and his colleagues produced. During his reign, Coltrane recorded more than most of his colleagues; in fact, he recorded more than did his predecessor Lester Young. This means that his records reached many more fans, as well as musicians, enabling him to exert a great deal more influence on both groups. (The more records and exposure an artist has, the more influence he has, and in many ways this is one of the ways that industry dictates the course of history.)

Perhaps Coltrane's most memorable impact on jazz was his recording of *My Favorite Things.* More than any other saxophonist during the 1960s, Coltrane almost singlehandedly reintroduced the soprano saxophone to jazz.

During this period, I had the great fortune of endorsing the Selmer saxophones and became personal friends with members of the Selmer family, George, Jacques and Jean, sons of the founder, Henri Selmer. On one of my monthly visits to the Selmer's Paris factory in Place Dancourt, George asked me why I thought the soprano had suddenly begun to sell in great numbers. I couldn't help but laugh because I knew that the increase in sales was primarily due to Coltrane's popular recording of *My Favorite Things.* Almost every saxophonist in jazz, after hearing Coltrane's recording, wanted to add the soprano to their repertoire of instruments.

My Favorite Things, a landmark recording, also emphasized Trane's interest in ethnic music, especially Arabic music and the music of India. During this period, many jazz musicians began to experiment with the use of third world music. In Coltrane's recording of *My Favorite Things,* he plays a number of phrases and scale lines that are closely related to various modes found in certain Indian ragas.

It was also during this time that Coltrane began his close relationship with one of India's greatest musicians, Ravi Shankar. Because of his enormous popularity, Coltrane influenced an entire generation of young musicians to look more closely at the ethnic music of Bahia, in northern Brazil, North Africa, Latin America, as well as East India.

John Coltrane's recording of *Africa* was another example of his interest in ethnic music. In Africa, various melodic and rhythm phrases lend themselves extensively to the music of West Africa. In this recording, avant-garde jazz musician Eric Dolphy is featured as an arranger and orchestrater, as well as performer, a role that surprised Dolphy's many critics, who were not sure that Dolphy could handle the delicate task of arranging and orchestrating the music for the date. The fact that Coltrane could and did use everything from classical to ethnic music in his work is further proof of his mastery of western music theory, especially in the area of jazz improvisation.

To understand the work of John Coltrane it is necessary first to examine the various periods of his career. The first period I refer to as his post bop period. Coltrane's first professional gigs as a jazz musician were played on alto saxophone. As with the majority of the great innovators during the 1940s and 1950s, Coltrane served his early apprenticeship in jazz as a player in various blues bands. One of the major differences between the so-called authentic jazz musician and the "school educated" jazz musician is the ability to play the blues. As the "little giant", tenor saxophonist, Johnny Griffin once advised me, "try to play the blues in everything you play" (personal interview with Johnny Griffin), and this philosophy is evident in Coltrane's playing, whether in a ballad or in the brilliant execution of a jazz standard.

According to fellow musicians and tenor saxophonists, Jimmy Heath and James Moody, it was not until he (Coltrane) joined the group of alto saxophonist Eddie "Clean Head" Vinson that Coltrane decided to switch from tenor to the alto saxophone, though on occasion he continued to play the alto. (During the late 1940s and 1950s, after having heard alto saxophonist Charley Parker, a number of saxophonists switched to tenor).

Once during a recording session in Paris for the O.R.T.F. (O.R.T.F. refers to the name of the French national radio/TV station), saxophonist Sonny Stitt told me that he and a number of other saxophonists had decided that "Bird" (Charlie Parker) had played just about everything that was possible on the alto—so they decided to change to tenor. During this period (1940s), established styles in the field of jazz were usually set by one or two players (Lester Young and Charlie Parker on saxophones or Dizzy Gillespie and Fats Navarrow on trumpets), and very few musicians deviated from that style.

When he joined the orchestra of trumpeter Dizzy Gillespie, Coltrane found himself in the company of one of the foremost innovators of all times. Unfortunately Coltrane's drug problem kept him from fully experiencing the benefits of a close relationship with Gillespie's brilliant musical mind. Nevertheless, Coltrane continued to grow and mature in Dizzy's big band.

Coltrane's solos during this period were still quite conventional—they were centered around the use of scales and extended chords. Tenor saxophonist, Jimmy Heath was introduced to John Coltrane by trumpeter, Bill Massey in 1946, shortly after Coltrane left the navy. Between 1947 and 1948, Jimmy invited Coltrane to join his band, and in 1949, both musicians worked together in the big band of trumpeter Dizzy Gillespie (personal interview with Jimmy Heath, 3/9/94).

Coltrane's period with Miles Davis found him deeply involved in extending the scope of his harmonic range by focusing on layers of sound rather than on chords or individual scales. (Round Midnight solo) In 1959, Coltrane left the Miles Davis group and was replaced by Jimmy Heath. (Interview with Jimmy Heath— October 1994)

Following his departure from the Miles Davis group, Coltrane's second major period centered around the formation of his now famous John Coltrane quartet, featuring McCoy Tyner, piano; Jimmy Garrison, acoustic bass; and Elvin Jones, drums. With this group, John Coltrane began his rise to jazz sainthood (recordings with *Crescent; Africa; Afro-Blue; Alabama; I Want to Talk About You; Your Lady*). Musically, Coltrane continued to experiment with the use of ethnic music as a medium of expression.

Throughout western European music history, major composers played a role in the interpretation of political events, e.g., Coltrane's sensitivity to the civil rights movement can be seen in compositions like *Alabama*. In many ways a quiet, soft-spoken man, Coltrane did not express his discontent in an open, hostile manner. Instead, he chose to express his discontentment with racial injustice through his music. Coltrane, as well as many of the great African American artists that preceded him, (e.g., Duke Ellington, Max Roach and Charlie Mingus) was extremely politically aware and contributed to the success of his political convictions in the way he knew best—through his music. Without doubt, Duke Ellington's *Black, Brown and Beige,* Max Roach's *Freedom Now Suite,* Charlie Mingus' *Fables of Faubus* are all examples of the political awareness that exists with jazz musicians.

The third and perhaps most controversial period of John Coltrane and his music took place during the mid-1960s with the composition of recordings such as *Ascension* (1965), in which Coltrane embraced the avant-garde. (Note: the true meaning of the term avant-garde as it applies to music of that period [1960s] according to the MerriamWebster dictionary, refers to "those especially in the arts who create or apply new or experimental ideas and techniques.")

The term avant-garde is relevant to its definition only in relationship to the time period in question. In other words, what would have been avant-garde in the 1920s might no longer have been considered avant-garde during the 1950s. Therefore, Coltrane's work of the 1960s existed in a world that witnessed the black youth of America rise in defiance of racial injustice and cultural assassination, where the effect of the civil rights marches throughout the major cities of the U.S. and the brutalization of those who participated in these marches made a lasting impression on Coltrane and his contemporaries. The

Charlie Parker. Archive Photos/Frank Driggs Collection.

impromptu striking of the drum or rare cry of the saxophone became synonymous with the movement.

Coltrane's rendition of classics like *A Love Supreme* and *Crescent* provides a penetrating glimpse of his inner religious and spiritual commitment. It is ironic that in many instances, spirituality is often associated with the traditional music of various ethnic groups. For some reason, in the United States, spirituality has often been overlooked when examining jazz, especially since African American music, in its most traditional form, is based on spirituality. Jazz and blues, as we know it today, both derive from early African American slave and religious songs borne out of protest and pain. The development of the music depended on one's spiritual relationship with God. Somehow, during the evolution of the music, this spirituality has been pushed into the background. What has emerged is a commercialism that perhaps developed from the economic games which have been associated with the music.

John Coltrane represented the conscience of black America. However, his music, regardless of ethnic origin, embraced all people and became a multicultural world-music. Through his music, he made the world aware of the African American struggle for liberation, peace and justice.

Thelonious Monk

Whenever the term genius is mentioned in connection with jazz, names like Charlie Parker, Art Tatum and Ray Charles readily come to mind; however, other artists of similar status also can and should be mentioned. Since the beginning of jazz, there have been self-proclaimed "greats," i.e., the reigning "emperor" of jazz. During the Dixieland period (also referred to as traditional New Orleans music), the majority of the elite jazz musicians were known as King (King Buddy Bolden, King Freddie Keppard, King Joe Oliver etc). Other groups used the word "original" to distinguish themselves, e.g., the "Original Tuxedo Jazz Band" or the "Original Dixieland Jazz Band," and later, such titles were applied to artists like Paul Whiteman, the "King of Jazz" or Benny Goodman the "King of Swing." Just who gave these musicians and their groups these "unofficial" titles are sometimes unknown; in many instances groups or their leaders bestowed these titles on themselves as advertising slogans.

At this point I will focus on the genius of Thelonius Monk as his ability to perceive and create music phenomena that is both innovative and artistically superior to the norms. First, let us look at the events in Monk's life that may have contributed to his status as a musical genius.

To say that Monk's music was unusual is an understatement. This became clear in a conversation with jazz saxophonist James Moody, who recounted to me his first performance with Monk. Moody had joined Dizzy Gillespie's band in 1947 for an engagement at the Spotlight Club on 52nd Street in New York City. During one of the numbers, Moody stood up to take a solo; to his surprise, instead of the structured chord changes usually associated with that particular composition, he heard only one note. It was Monk, who was seated at the piano. The other members of the rhythm section (Kenny Clarke, drums; Milt Jackson, vibes; Ray Brown, bass) kept on playing without missing a beat. At that point, Moody said, "I knew that I was on my own, so I just closed my eyes and kept on wailing."

According to jazz pianist Billy Taylor, "Thelonius Monk was one of the original rebels of the bebop era, but his talents as a composer-pianist were now beginning to come into focus. Musicians admired him and worked hard to learn his music. Yet he was passed over by the critics and the general public until Orin Keepnews and Bill Grauer began to record him for the Riverside label during the 1950s." (*Jazz Piano History and Development,* Billy Taylor. William C. Brown Co. publishers, pg. 168–169)

In 1963, my wife Ursula, stride pianist Joe Turner, and I attended a concert in Paris at the Salle Playell featuring Thelonius Monk and his group. During the concert, Monk was improvising at the piano when he suddenly jumped up and began dancing to the music of his group. At that moment Joe Turner turned to me and said, "I used to know that ole boy when he was really playing—man, he could really play. That was before he started dancing and acting strange." Years later, when I began to lecture on jazz, I thought about Joe's comments. Had Monk forsaken improvisation in favor of entertainment or was there another reason for his dancing and unusual stage mannerisms that was not evident to the outsider? I prefer to choose the latter, i.e., that Monk had become so engrossed in his music that he felt the need to express his feelings by doing what came naturally—dancing. After all, jazz in its earliest form was a dance music, and it was not until much later that it became a concert music.

Thelonius Monk was perhaps the most influential modern pianist during the bebop and postbebop era. "Parallel to Charlie Parker it is Thelonius Monk that the modern pianists have borrowed the most from in order to create a new style." (*Jazz Solfeges* by Andre Francis, Editions Du Seuil France, pg. 112) Jazz drummer, Art Blakey, may have best illustrated the jazz musician's admiration for the contributions of Thelonius Monk when he said "Monk is the guy who started it all; he came before both Parker and Gillespie."(*The Encyclopedia of Jazz* by Leonard Feather, a Da Capo paperback) This statement is worth noting because Blakey, a major drummer, band leader and innovator, was also known for his ability to predict and showcase the most promising new jazz talent. However, even with Blakey's endorsement, for years Monk was overlooked by many jazz critics as well as the general public. His peers, however, continued to support his musical genius and eventually helped him to win the recognition that he finally received.

Monk's music was ahead of his time. As German jazz scholar and writer Joachim Berendt wrote:

> "Much of what leads to Ornette Coleman, John Coltrane, Eric Dolphy, and all the other avant-gardists of jazz is heard for the first time in his (Monk's) music-anchored in a strong blues feeling and saturated with a mocking, burlesquing sense of humor. Monk's own themes, with their rhythmic displacements and irregular structures, were the most original themes on the Jazz scene of the fifties." (*The Jazz Book,* J. Berendt; translation: Dan Morgenstern, Helmutt Barbara Bredigkit, Lawrence Hill & Co.)

Monk, one of jazz's most prolific performers, has been criticized for his lack of technique. This is inaccurate. Monk's technique was practical and he was very knowledgeable in balancing technique and phrasing. In many of his compositions, e.g., *Twinkle, Twinkle,* it is apparent that a melody so complex and diverse required considerable ability and theoretical knowledge to execute it. The fact that Monk did not play with a great deal of speed or technique in every song is attributed to the fact that he felt that certain types of techniques should be used in support of specific musical ideas.

Monk was a cerebral musician. He was constantly thinking about music and its place in art, and trying to find new ways to express his ideas. According to musicians close to him, Monk was so absorbed in his music that he would actually walk around the house, sometimes for weeks at a time, without communicating with his family. He was preoccupied with the sorting out of various musical ideas and solving these problems so that he could perform them with his group.

A close examination of Monk's music reveals a certain logic to his work; every phrase and musical idea has a specific function, e.g., the composition *Round Midnight.* The construction of phrases and the position of the melody in the overall harmonic structure is creative, unique and musically sound. Each and every note has a definite function and plays an essential role in balancing the structure of the piece. Monk's use of angular and irregular rhythms (i.e., rhythms that occur in uncommon places and on uncommon beats in the music) shows another side of his musical thinking. A good example of this can be found in the blues composition *Straight, No Chaser.*

Example R.A.-VII displays an 8 measure theme in the style of pianist and composer Thelonius Monk and is based on the two bar melodic phrase. In the 1st two measures we find the interval of a Major 6th which constitutes the main melodic figure. Measure two (2) starts on B natural which is a 1/2 step below the C (first note of the first measure). Measure 3 introduces a new melodic motif by introducing minor 2nds throughout measure 4. Measures 5 and

R.A. VII In the style of Monk

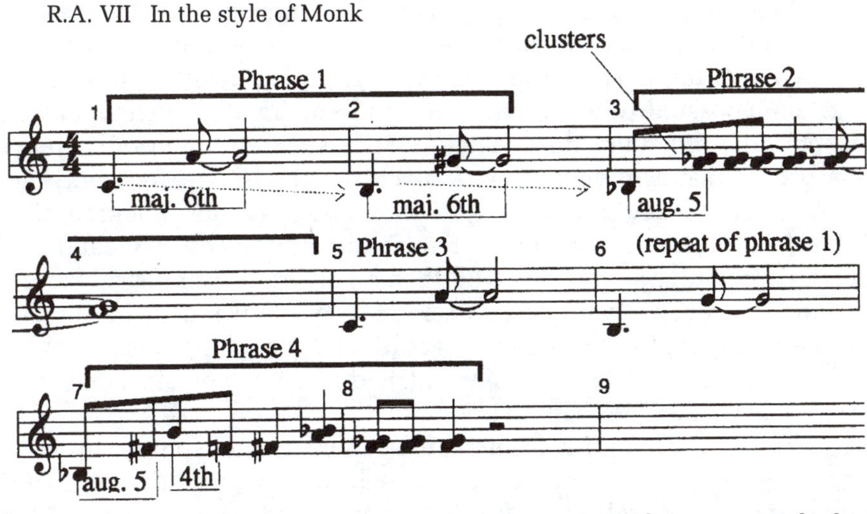

Computerized music examples by
Mary Ann Morroco

6 repeat the principal themes introduced in measures 1 and 2. In measure 7 we find a leap of an augmented 5th followed by an interval of a Major 3rd (F# to A# or Bb), followed by a descending leap from Bb to F natural. The F occurs on the up beat and advances to F# which then progresses to a typical 1/2 step Monk-type cluster. The final melodic statement then comes to an end with a series of three 1/2 two note step clusters on Gb and F.

Neither of these compositions, *Round Midnight or Straight, No Chaser,* requires a great deal of advanced technical proficiency to perform, but they do require a certain intellectual approach to be interpreted correctly.

The idea of space or silence in music is also very germane and essential to successfully and properly interpret a piece such as *Round Midnight.* Monk was not the first of his generation to utilize the concept of space in music. Both classical and jazz improvisationalists have previously used this technique, and Count Basie and Lester Young used the technique of space and/or silence quite effectively in their music.

According to Monk, space was just as much an integral part of music as were the notes. He felt that the planning of a composition should involve the use of space in relation to the selection of notes for each musical idea or phrase. Why did Monk have such adamant feelings about the use of space in his musical compositions? Perhaps this was his way of referring to music as a direct and conclusive extension of nature. If music represents the immediate environment and space and silence are a part of this environment, then silence and space must be included in a definition of music. Music is a definite composite of melody, harmony and rhythm, and rhythm is measured in relationship to time. Therefore, space or silence must be included in our definition of music, for without space there would be no time, and thus no music.

The alteration of rhythms combined with the use of space was one of Monk's trademarks. During the bebop period, his expansion of harmonic concepts through his clever, but practical usage of such altered notes as the flatted 5th, raised elevenths and flat thirteenths was as impressive as his sometimes angular melodies. The use of such altered extensions required a tremendous amount of discipline and a thorough knowledge and understanding of the various harmonic possibilities that exist within the realm of a given tonal area.

There are numerous controversial stories surrounding Monk's playing, especially ones that involve musicians like Miles Davis, who frequently asked Monk to "stroll" or lay out, during a Davis solo. My interpretation of such stories is that Monk actually preferred to lay out, and to absorb what the other musicians were doing so that he could then reconstruct his musical ideas into a new and more musically provocative creation, as many musicians during the bebop era would do. Classical composers like Haydn, Chopin and Mozart often utilized this method, creating new music through the musical extension of the original basic melodic patterns.

The music of Thelonius Monk can be looked at as simple, in terms of thematic material (except for the more technical pieces such as *Twinkle, Twinkle*), or as a cerebral, beautiful, yet complicated musical thesis. Monk's work often has been described as a body of music that follows the path to perfection by choosing the most musical road to simplicity. This kind of simplicity, however, requires various degrees of intellectual, technical and spiritual development. This idea of reaching creative perfection through simplicity is also very prominent in the work of such artists as Lester Young and Miles Davis.

Another important element of music is actually experiencing the music that one plays (or at least experiencing the aesthetic values surrounding the climate in which one performs), and living one's music was very prominent during the bebop period. Thelonius Monk, Charlie Parker, Dizzy Gillespie, Bud Powell, and others, all preached this philosophy—living a particular life style in order to play "real" jazz. The typical negative portrait of the jazz musician refers not only to the use of drugs and/or any other negative activity as often reported by the media, but also to the special bond that developed between individuals or groups who shared the same, common experiences, e.g., jamming together. These common experiences may have inspired jazz musicians to think in a similar way and eventually to play in a similar way.

Another controversy among jazz artists during the bebop era focused on the legality and copyright of original compositions performed—The question was, who actually composed the songs that many of the artists recorded? Tunes such as *Tune Up* by Miles Davis and *Epistrophy* by Thelonius Monk fall into this category. For example, drummer Kenny Clarke pointed out to me that he, and not Monk, had composed *Epistrophy.* He showed me the composition title sheet from SACEM (the French agency, similar to ASCAP in the U.S., that was responsible for collecting royalties for composers and authors). A thorough examination of SACEM's records showed that Kenny Clarke was indeed receiving royalties as the composer of *Epistrophy.* However, according to Ursula Davis in her book *Paris Without Regret* (University of Iowa Press), Monk and Kenny collaborated on *Epistrophy,* one of the first modern jazz originals. (*Paris Without Regret,* p. 49)

Historian Leonard Feather states in *The Encyclopedia of Jazz* that Thelonius Monk was born in Rocky Mount, North Carolina on October 10, 1920. "At the age of four, Thelonius moved with his parents to a Manhattan neighborhood known as San Juan Hill" (*Introduction to Jazz History* by Donald D. Megil and Richard S. Demory, Prentice Hall, p. 155) Monk was a self-taught musician. Perhaps his early experience as a pianist, touring with a sanctified evangelist and playing for healing services, was responsible for his gospel/blueslike soulful approach to music.

(The presence of blues or gospel in jazz, especially during the bebop and hardbop years, suggests that jazz derived from the same African American plantation experience that produced early blues, gospels and spirituals. The essence of jazz then stems from the assimilation of Western African and Western European cultures in the U.S.)

Monk's music was as complicated as the man himself—music was his life and his life was his music, and he used music as his way of relating to the world. French writer and jazz critic, Francis Hofstein, writing in *The International Jazz Journal* (Vol. I, No. I, pg. 56, University of Pittsburgh Hall of Fame Publication) stated:

> "To Monk, however, the boundaries he voluntarily assigned to his repertoire, the relentless quest that indisputably drove him to find and, above all, that extraordinary sense of time that bring him, whatever the interval between two notes, the length of a silence, or the melodic or harmonic line played by a soloist (Milt Jackson for example), to always be in place in an exactness and a rhythmic mastery which have little equivalence in Jazz, could have permitted him, in the same way he broke on stage or on record, succeeding just at the right moment to restore presence, consistency and pertinence to the music, to fail also in place in his life."

Monk, in a sense, was a master at the art of "cultural surgery", the reconstruction and reidentification of newly formed, artistic modules. He fused together these various artistic modules into a highly provocative and intellectual form, a form so transformed that few, if any, recognized them in their final stage. They were, in fact, new.

> "man behaves in this manner, as Hegel writes, in the name of his freedom of subject, to remove from the outside world its fiercely strange and foreign nature and to enjoy things only because he finds there the outside form of his own reality, when congruence, at least relative, between outside and inside does not precisely fail." (International Archives Journal Vol. I, No. I, p. 56) (Francis Hofstein International Jazz Archives Journal)

In many ways Hofstein, in this statement, is referring to Monk and his approach to his art. Monk was one of the least copied of all the pianists in jazz history. Why? Is it because his music was so distant from its original source (i.e., the various styles of jazz that preceded his music—swing, rag, etc.), that his contemporaries chose not to duplicate his music? Or was his music so unique in terms of form and structure, that it was virtually impossible to accurately reproduce it?

The answer to this complex question is somewhere in between. Monk's music was different from his contemporaries and many of them chose to forego the almost impossible task of trying to reproduce it. However, there are many jazz pianists who quote Monk in their work (Dollar Brand, Cecil Taylor, Walter Davis, Michael Mikkelburg, Geri Allen, George Cables, Don Pullen, including horn players such as Johnny Griffin and Steve Lacy on saxophone and Don Cherry on trumpet). These pianists, instrumentalists, composers and arrangers found Monk's music not only stimulating but also futuristic.

The final irony for those who feel that Monk's music is weird or "outside" (as some writers have stated), is the "kinship" that his music shares with Duke Ellington's—whose music was not considered weird. A close examination of Duke's performance supports this theory.

9 African American Composers in the Western European Art Tradition

When referring to the music of African Americans, the sounds of hard-driving Gospels, emotional spirituals, hot buttered blues or swinging jazz readily comes to mind. Yet many African American composers have chosen to compose and perform classical music, and to varying degrees these composers and performers, past and present, have been left out of the mainstream of individuals designated as major composers. For example, early composers such as William Grant Still, Ulysses Kay, William Dawson, Samuel Coleridge Taylor, Hale Smith, Harry Burleigh, Clarence Cameron White, Nathaniel Dett, Howard Swanson, Will Marion Cook and Julia Perry, etc. (*The Music of Black Americans,* E. Southern, W.W. Norton and Company) were virtually unknown to the majority of African American music lovers. Their music, regardless of cultural and thematic origin, was to many African Americans an attempt to imitate the music of white society. In fact, these composers would not have been able to survive without the support of numerous societies or social groups (frequently associated with the African American church) who sponsored their concerts.

These early African American composers laid the groundwork for the next generation of African American composers, who found it even more of a challenge to compose music in a tradition that was looked upon as anti-black or "white folks" music by their fellow African Americans. Younger composers like Olly Wilson, David Baker, Noel de Costa, T. J. Anderson, Frederick Tillus, Wendell Logan, Coleridge Taylor Perkinson, William Bill Fischer, Anthony Davis, Alvin Singleton, Donald Byrd, Jimmy Heath and Benny Golson were able to find not only an audience for their music, but also the moral justification and cultural support needed for composing in a tradition that was culturally foreign. These composers were musically and socially invisible to their fellow African Americans, who felt it was impossible to compose music of any substance unless it accurately reflected the African American's cultural milieu.

Many African American composers studied either at non-traditional African American institutions or privately with European composers. Schools like the New England Conservatory of Music, Chicago Musical College, The American Conservatory of Music (Chicago), Teachers College of Columbia

Wendell Logan. Muzimu Music, Inc.

Olly Wilson. Ed Kirwan Graphic Arts.

Benny Golson and Art Farmer. Archive Photos.

University, Yale University, Oberlin College, Fisk University, Wilberforce University (Ohio) and Howard University were responsible for training many early African American composers. Black music scholar Eileen Southern, in her treatise *The Music of Black Americans,* states:

> "Oscar Anderson Fuller (singer and composer) was the first to earn a Ph.D. in music in the United States. He received a master's degree in music from the State University of Iowa in 1934 and the doctorate from the same university in 1942 with a major in composition." (Southern, p. 452)

Perhaps the first indication of the African American's interest in performing classical music occurred on the plantation when slaves, some at the urging or insistence of their slave owners, performed at social gatherings. Newspapers and posters that advertised slaves for sale often highlighted the slave's ability to perform on the fiddle or other instruments, such as the guitar, calabasse and jews harp. Many slaves, before being abducted and transported to the colonies, were skilled iron workers and wood carvers who probably crafted various musical instruments out of iron and other metals.

The assumption that Africans were skilled only in the art of making drums from the bark of trees and goat's skin and performing only on the drums is inaccurate. Evidence of the African slaves' literacy in music can be seen in Eileen Southern's account of African slaves attending college with their owners.

> "Students took their slaves with them to College of William and Mary in Williamsburg (established in 1693). Some contemporaries thought it unfortunate that there were not special quarters for blacks, similar to the (apartment) for Indians. There is very great occasion for a quarter for the Negroes

and inferior servants belonging to the college, wrote Hugh Jones in 1724. For the slaves, however, the circumstance was fortunate; they lived in rooms of their young masters and undoubtedly attended classes with them on various occasions. More than likely, many a slave at the college learned to play very well on the Violin or to play extremely well on the french horn from attending music classes at the college, which were taught by masters from the town rather than by members of the regular faculty." (Southern, p. 63, *The Music of Black Americans,* W.W. Norton)

This analysis suggests that slaves benefited from attending classes with their masters and that they also received expert training from the visiting masters who presented classes at the school. This experience indicates that slaves were well trained in classical music.

Another issue concerning African American music is the question of authenticity. Was the music of these talented individuals African American because the composers were themselves African American? Or is race the only or major criteria that predetermines the type or style of a composition? If the answer to these questions is yes, then nationality or race should be eliminated when studying the work of the native composer who lives and composes in another country. For example, was Frederic Chopin, whose father was French, a French composer? Or was he a Polish composer who later migrated to Paris? A composer's particular ethnic background does not determine the ethnicity of his/her work; factors such as cultural experience, education and social acceptance, all play an important role in determining the essence and validity of a composition.

Hildred Roach, in *Black American Music: Past and Present,* identified a number of composers of African American origin—outside the United States—who were responsible for enriching the musical life and vocabulary of their respective countries, including Jose Mauricio and Claudia Jose as well as Domingo Brendes de Sala, a musician from Cuba during the 1800s. In addition, Roach mentions Ludovic Lamothe, The black Chopin, a musician of Haitian decent who composed numerous waltzes and other classical pieces, and Nunes Garcia, who was born in Brazil of mixed Indian and Negro heritage, who was an organist and choirmaster. These individuals represent only a few unsung composers of African and Latin heritage who contributed greatly to the repertoire of the international music scene (Roach, pp. 278-290).

These composers—of African or mixed heritage—excelled in the world of classical music. Obviously, it was not skin color but social, economic and artistic conditions, and opportunity, that launched a composer's work. If the composer of color works in a hostile environment, he ceases to create. This, along with not being given ample opportunity to present his work in a proper setting, makes the work of such composers obscure to the memories as well as history books of the world. Thus, we find the comparable artists in the United States having their work performed within the underground cultural network that existed in the U.S., namely: The many social and artistic cultural organizations that existed during the Harlem Renaissance, the black church and other venues throughout the African American community.

According to author Hildred Roach, the composer George Augustus Polgreen Bridgetower, thought to have been the inspiration for Beethoven's

Kreutzer Sonata for Violin (one of the most monumental and technically challenging works ever written for the violin), was a child prodigy who began his performing career at the age of ten. Young Bridgetower rapidly developed a reputation as a virtuoso on the violin. Many composers often get their inspiration from virtuoso players and Bridgetower's influence on a major figure like Beethoven, in my estimation, makes him a major contributor to the great classical repertoire of that period. (*Black American Music: Past and Present,* Krieger Publishing Company.)

Another interesting point of comparison regarding classical composers is the relationship between composers of African descent born in the U.S. and those of mixed blood who were born outside the U.S., e.g., Jose White. Jose (Joseph) White was a native of Cuba. At an early age, he entered the conservatory at Paris where he repeatedly won prizes for his skill in playing the violin. In Europe, White was reputed to be "one of the most distinguished violinists of the French school" and also "a composer of note." (Southern, *The Music of Black Americans,* p. 256)

Another significant group to consider are composer-performers of African descent who studied, worked and remained in Europe for a considerable length of time, or who were actually Euro-Africans. Samuel Coleridge Taylor, a British composer with an African father and English mother, was one of Europe's premier composers; his enormous output has been well documented in the U.S. and in Europe. In the case of both Bridgetower and Taylor, the question is should they be considered African American composers or should they be referred to as Euro-African composers? (I must admit that I have not personally seen this latter term in any of the scholarly writings that I have examined, but I am certain that the term, if not already in use, will soon become an accepted term for such musicians.)

Composers and performers of African-European and Latin heritage offer another example of the variety of ethnic cultural and musical contributions to world music. Although the music of Bridgetower and Coleridge Taylor is basically European, Coleridge Taylor was fascinated with the blues and other forms of African American music; however, it is not clear if this influence permeated his music. On the other hand, Bridgetower's music was definitely European, regardless of his African heritage. Bridgetower may have attempted to borrow music from other cultures, as did other musicians of this period, but the fact remains that when one hears this music its influence is primarily European, not African American. In the case of Bridgetower, who was born in Poland, educated in Europe and performed in Germany, England and Russia, it is evident that he was influenced by other black intellectuals of mixed heritage. (Roach-Southern)

In Europe during the 1800s, a group of highly educated blacks or mixed bloods served as the nucleus of a black pseudo-intelligentsia. Many of the Euro-African intellectuals (who originally came to Europe as indentured servants of French and Russian elite) had studied at prestigious European institutions such as the famous Conservatory National of Music and the Sorbonne (University of Paris). According to reliable sources these individuals of mixed heritage often met to discuss their work and the important issues of the day similar to the famous intellectuals (Les Six) who met in Paris to discuss their art.

"Les Six" was a group of French composers consisting of Arthur Honegger, Darius Milhaud, Francis Poulenc, Louis Durey, George Auric and Germaine Taillefaire, who under the guidance of composer Erik Satie and writer/philosopher Jean Colteau met on a consistent basis to discuss and eventually to perform each other's music. Milhaud states:

> After a concert at the Salle Huyghens (in 1919), at which Bertin sang Louis Durey's *Images a Crusoe* on words by Saint-Leger and the Capella Quartet played by "Fourth Quartet," the critic Henri Collet published in "Comoedia," a chronicle entitled "Five Russians and Six Frenchmen." Quite arbitrarily he had chosen six names: Auric, Durey, Honegger, Poulenc, Taillefaire, and my own, merely because we knew each other, were good friends, and figured on the same programs; quite irrespective of our different temperaments and wholly dissimilar characters. (*Composers on Music, An Anthology of Composers Writings from Palestrina to Copeland.* Edited by Sam Morganstern, Pantheon Books, p. 475.)

Another important African American musician-composer is the brilliant Dean Dixon. (When I lived in Europe [1961–69], I was reminded frequently of Dixon's genius whenever I accepted a recording or concert date at one of the European state-run radio stations.) According to European musicians like German trombonist, Albert Mangelsdorf and African American conductor, George Byrd (whom I had the distinct pleasure of working with in Salvador Bahia in the Northeastern section of Brazil), Dixon was not only a brilliant conductor-composer but also a complete musician—a multi-instrumentalist and composer. One of Dixon's strengths as a musician was his ability to perform brilliantly on every instrument in the orchestra. If he was not satisfied with the way one of the orchestra members was performing a particular part, he would simply take the instrument oboe, bassoon, violin, cello, timpani, etc. and personally demonstrate just how he expected the part to be played. As a conductor, his colleagues thought he was brilliant. According to Raoul Abdul in his book *Blacks in Classical Music,* Dean trained as a composer at Julliard School of Music, where he received a B.S. and at Columbia Teachers College, where he received his M.A. In 1948, unable to obtain work as a first- rate con-

Dean Dixon. Archive Photos/Frank Driggs Collection.

ductor or musical director of a major American orchestra, Dixon left for Europe, where he became the musical director of the Goteborg Symphony orchestra in Sweden (1953–1960). In 1961, he was appointed musical director of the Hessischer Rundfunk Orchestra in Frankfurt am Main, in Germany. (*Blacks in Classical Music,* p. 192).

Perhaps the most respected African American composer of classical music was William Grant Still. Still, born in Woodville, Mississippi, on May 11, 1895, credits his parents, William Grant and Carrie Leana Prambro Still, with providing the early influence found in his music. Often referred to as the "dean of African American composers," Still's work ranged from the jazz of his early student days at Wilberforce University to his commercial orchestrations for Black Swan Records, and his critically acclaimed Afro-American Symphony. (*William Grant Still,* R. B. Haas, Black Sparrow Press)

Still's ability to take advantage of the hollow, almost eerie sound of the English horn is a brilliant example of using color and texture, and in the very first measures of his work Afro American Symphony, he skillfully introduces the English horn for this very purpose. Only the faint tapping sound of a timpani, accompanied by the harp and strings, interrupt this deep mysterious African-like atmosphere.

In measure 7, Part I, 4th beat, he sets the stage for the blues-like entrance of the 1st trumpet solo by having the Bass Clarinet play a low glissando-like figure beginning on low F proceeding up to (Bb). The trumpet then enters with a whining blues-like solo reminiscent of the human-like sound of Bubber Miley during his years with the Duke Ellington Orchestra.

For those critics who further question the authenticity of Still's work and its relationship to jazz, a careful examination of the horn shout in measures 2,

William Grant Still. Archive Photos.

ORCHESTRATION

3 Flutes (3rd doubling Piccolo)
2 Oboes
English Horn
2 Clarinets in B flat
Bass Clarinet
2 Bassoons

4 Horns in F
3 Trumpets in B flat
3 Tenor Trombones
Tuba

Percussion (3 players):

- Timpani
- Vibraphone
- Triangle
- Wire Brush
- Small Cymbal
- Cymbals
- Snare Drum
- Bass Drum
- Gong
- Bells

Celeste
Harp
Tenor Banjo

Strings

DURATION 23¾ MINUTES

Part 1: 7¼ minutes *Part 3: 4 minutes*
Part 2: 5¼ minutes *Part 4: 7¼ minutes*

With humble thanks to God, the source of inspiration

William Grant Still

1 Moderato assai

'All my life long twell de night has pas'
Let de wo'k come ez it will,
So dat I fin' you, my honey, at last',
Somewhaih des ovah de hill.'

Paul Laurence Dunbar

2 Adagio

'It's moughty tiahsome layin' 'roun'
Dis sorrer-laden earfly groun',
An' oftentimes I thinks, thinks I
'Twould be a sweet t'ing des to die
An' go 'long home.'

Paul Laurence Dunbar

3 Animato

'An' we'll shout ouah halleluyahs,
On dat mighty reck'nin' day.'

Paul Laurence Dunbar

4 Lento, con risoluzione

'Be proud, my Race, in mind and soul.
Thy name is writ on Glory's scroll
In characters of fire..
High mid the clouds of Fame's bright sky
Thy banner's blazoned folds now fly,
And truth shall lift them higher.'

Paul Laurence Dunbar

He who develops his God-given gifts with view to aiding humanity, manifests truth.

MODERATO ASSAI - 𝅗𝅥 = 88
AFRO-AMERICAN SYMPHONY
- I -
William Grant Still
1
ENG. HORN
TIMPANI
HARP
1ST. VLNS.
2ND. VLNS.
VIOLAS
'CELLI
BASSES
SOLO
legato
poco accel.
ritard.
a Tempo
riten.
pizz.
OBOE
ENGLISH HRN.
CLARINET
BASS CLAR.
BASSOON
HORN
TRUMPET
TROMBONE
TIMPANI
SMALL CYMBAL
BASS DRUM
HARP
1ST. VLNS.
2ND. VLNS.
VIOLAS
'CELLI
BASSES
Harmon mute
Soft stick
cresc
MADE IN ENGLAND

OBOE 1 2
ENG. HORN
CLARINET 1 2
PASS CLAR.
BASSOON 1 2
HORN 1 2 3 4
TRUMPET 1
TIMPANI
SMALL CYMB.
BASS DRUM
damped
HARP
1ST. VLNS.
2ND. VLNS.
VIOLAS
'CELLI
BASSES

3
FLUTE 1 2
OBOE 1 2
ENG. HORN
SOLO
CLARINET 1 2
BASS CLAR.
BASSOON 1 2
HORN 1 2 3 4
TRUMPET 1
TIMPANI
damped
SMALL CYMB.
BASS DR.
HARP
1ST. VLNS
2ND. VLNS
VIOLAS
'CELLI
BASSES
spicc.
arco
pizz.
3

FLUTE
PICCOLO
OBOE 1
CLARINET
SOLO
HARP
1ST.VLNS.
2ND.VLNS.
VIOLAS
'CELLI
BASSES
rit. poco a poco
stacc.
OBOE 2
BASSOON
pizz.

PIU MOSSO - 𝅗𝅥 = 112
accel.
4
FLUTE 1 2
PICCOLO
OBOE 1 2
Col 1st Oboe
ENG. HORN
CLARINET 1 2
BASS CLAR.
BASSOON 1 2
rit.
accel.
HORN 1 2 3 4
TRUMPETS
TROMBONES
TUBA
TIMPANI
CYMBALS
HARP
1ST. VLNS.
2ND. VLNS.
VIOLAS
'CELLI
BASSES
arco
Col 1st
accel.
4 PIU MOSSO - 𝅗𝅥 = 112

rit.
FLUTE 1 2
PICCOLO
OBOE 1 2
ENG. HORN
CLARINET 1 2
BASS CLAR.
BASSOON 1 2
HORN 1 2 3 4
senza sord.
TRUMPET 1 2
TROMBONE 1 2 3
senza sord.
TUBA
TIMPANI
TRIANGLE
CYMBALS
DRUMS
HARP
1ST VLNS.
2ND VLNS.
VIOLAS
'CELLI
BASSES
pizz.

ANDANTE CANTABILE - 𝅗𝅥 = 72
7
poco - - - a - - - poco
FLUTE 1
OBOE 1
CLARINET 1
BASS CLAR.
HORN 1
HARP
1ST. VLNS.
2ND. VLNS.
VIOLAS
'CELLI
BASSES
SOLO
teneramente
div.
FLUTE 1
OBOE
CLARINET 1
BASS CLAR.
HORN
TIMPANI
VIBRAPHONE
HARP
1ST. VLNS.
2ND. VLNS.
VIOLAS
'CELLI
BASSES
rit.
UN POCO PIU LENTO
accel.
POCO PIU MOSSO
tenute
SOLO
SOLI
2 Solo Violins
All of the Vlns.
f passionato
legatissimo
legatiss.

COME PRIMA
rall.
SOLO
FLUTE
ENG. HORN
CLARINET 1
BASS CLAR.
HORN
TIMPANI
CELESTA
1ST. VLNS.
2ND. VLNS.
VIOLAS
'CELLI
BASSES
dolce
div.
7
Ch. to PICCOLO
BASSOON
HORN 1
HARP
tenuto
SOLI
ardente
normal position
(*) With nails, and close to the sounding board.
A.A.S.

9
PIU MOSSO (non tanto)
poco riten. 8 accel. poco a poco sin al Allegro
FLUTES
PICCOLO
CLARINET 1 2
BASS CLAR.
BASSOON 1 2
poco riten. accel. poco a poco sin al Allegro
HORN 1 2 3 4
TRUMPET 1 2 3
senza sord.
TROMBONE 1 2 3
TUBA
poco riten. accel. poco a poco sin al Allegro
TIMPANI
G - B♮ - E♭
SUSP. CYMBAL
damped
damp quickly
HARP
poco riten.
poco riten. accel. poco a poco sin al Allegro
1ST. VLNS.
2ND. VLNS.
VIOLAS
'CELLI
BASSES
sonore
8 PIU MOSSO (non tanto)

20
9 ALLEGRO - 𝅗𝅥 = 160
A2
FLUTE 1 2
PICCOLO
OBOE 1 2
CLARINET 1 2
BASS CLAR.
BASSOON 1 2
HORN 1 2 3 4
Bells up
TRUMPET 1 2 3
Harmon Mutes
TROMBONE 1 2 3
stacc.
TUB
TIMPANI
Ab - B♮ - E♭
CYMBALS
S. DRUM.
HARP
1ST. VLNS
2ND. VLNS
VIOLAS
'CELLI
BASSES.
pizz.
9 ALLEGRO - 𝅗𝅥 = 160

3 and 4 and its relationship to the syncopated off-beat accents found in the double reeds is evident of his allegiance to jazz.

(Early in my academic career [1970] as an assistant professor of music at the University of Pittsburgh, I often found myself engaged in deep and often heated conversations with members of the composition faculty regarding the question of what constituted an American style of composition. Because I had spent so many years living in Europe, mainly Paris, I was convinced that music [classical or art music] written by American-born composers, regardless of whether the composer was African American, Euro-American, etc., was primarily Western European art music written by an American. My colleagues, quite naturally, had adopted the opposite position—that the music that they were writing was, in every way, representative of a new American school of composition.)

"The fact that Still's racial background was so diverse (Negro, Indian, Spanish, and Irish on his mother's side and Scotch, Negro and Choctaw Indian on his father's side) makes him the quintessential all-American composer. On his own (on occasion) he has added the Creole idiom of French Louisiana and the Hebraic as he learned it through his commission undertaken for the Park Avenue Synagogue." (*William Grant Still* edited by Robert Bardett Haas, Black Sparrow Press p.1)

The idea that one composer, regardless of ethnic origin, could offer such a vast and diversified cultural contribution to the world of music is staggering. Still's experience with popular music at Wilberforce University and his later work as an arranger for notable popular figures like Paul Whiteman, Sophie Tucker and Artie Shaw, together with his commercial work as a performer on the cello, clarinet, oboe and as an arranger, orchestrater and composer provided him with a highly diversified musical background, rarely matched by any of his contemporaries.

Given the range of his artistic and professional experience, William Grant Still should indeed be viewed as one of music history's master composers; his musical virtuosity enabled him to achieve a wealth of academic, artistic, creative and intellectual skills. His study at Wilberforce and later at Oberlin College, as well as his private studies with George Chadwick (*W. G. Still*, Haas. p.6) and the noted French composer Edgar Varese, also provided him with a solid foundation and insight into the avant-garde of this period.

Ulysses Kay, born in Tucson, Arizona (*Blacks in Classical Music,* R. Abdul, Dodd Mead Co.), is another African American composer who distinguished himself as a classical composer. According to Eileen Southern in The Music of Black Americans (W. Norton Co.), "The majority of Kay's works are written in the traditional forms: overtures, concertos, suites, symphonies, quartets, and cantatas. (p. 469) In *Black American Music: Past and Present* (2nd edition), Hildred Roach states:

> "Even though a good many of Kay's works are of the neo-Baroque tradition in contrapuntal features and forms, much of that which has gone before reflects the classical period in form."

Again, similar to the varied background of W. G. Still, Kay's diverse experience as a violinist, pianist and saxophonist as well as a composer of popular music, appears to have provided him with a wide breadth of musical nuances that resulted in a rich, diversified, truly American style of composition. This diversification has been the most significant musical ingredient that separates the African American composer from his European counterpart. The use of Negro spirituals, gospels, blues and work songs, in addition to the already established forms such as the sonata, concerto and symphony, resulted in a culturally enriched musical composition that was unique.

Hale Smith is one of the most prolific of the African American Composers living today (1990s) who composes in the Western European Tradition. His past experience as an arranger for some of the more established Jazz groups on the scene has provided him with a diversified and highly eclectic approach to composition. "In the field of Jazz, Smith has arranged for Chico Hamilton, Oliver Nelson, Quincy Jones, Eric Dolphy, Ahmad Jamal and others." (*Black American Music: Past and Present*, H. Roach, p. 215, Krieger Publishing Company)

His skillful use of Jazz rhythms and almost haunting-like approach to melodic development is both unique and artistically challenging.

Harry T. Burleigh, according to Eileen Southern in *The Music of Black Americans* was the earliest of the Black nationalist composers (p. 284). Burleigh was from Erie, Pennsylvania. He had an unusual musical background during his early years, gaining valuable experience by singing in the various churches in and around the area. His formal training included study at the National Conservatory and private study with Anton Dvorak. Burleigh influenced the work of composer Anton Dvorak by singing Negro spirituals for the composer. A singer of extraordinary talent, Burleigh's musical experience as soloist at Temple Emmanuel and St. George's Episcopal Church provided him with yet another source of musical inspiration for his work as a composer.

In studying the lives of the numerous African American classical composers it appears that they generally are more diversified in their training than their European counterparts, and tend to express this diversification in their music. The fusing of Spanish music with Caribbean (Jamaica, Trinidad, Martinque, Guadelope, etc.), African American blues and gospels, and Hungarian, French or German songs is both stimulating and invigorating.

Another aspect of African American music is the African American jazz musician who pursued his interest in composition by performing and composing classical music; this has been one of the most interesting changes to occur among young African American composers since 1950. African American jazz musicians who also compose Western European traditional music tend to be musicians who have had a considerable amount of experience in small group improvisation, an approach which they include in their work. Examples of such artists include: Jimmy Heath, Benny Golson, Max Roach, John Lewis (Modern Jazz Quartet); pianist Mary Tucker; trumpeter Donald Byrd; trombonist Slide Hampton; composer Wendell Logan; pianist Geri Allen, etc.

In recent years I have also written several compositions in the Western European Art musical tradition utilizing jazz improvisational techniques embedded within the fabric of the work. Evidence of this can be seen in works

Harry T. Burleigh. Photographer: Mishkin Studio, N.Y., Schomburg Center for Research in Black Culture.

such as my "Symphony for Orchestra and Jazz Saxophone" (dedicated to John F. Kennedy, Jr. and commissioned by Belgium Radio T.V. and Elias Gistelinck), also "Piece for Solo Violin" (premiered at the University of Pittsburgh's Frick Fine Arts Auditorium by Belgium violinist Jenny Spanogue), and most recently an opera entitled "Just Above My Head" which is based on an adaptation of the novel of the same name from author James Baldwin. (The adaptation of James Baldwin's "Just Above My Head" was written by Dr. Ursula Broschke Davis, Penn State University.)

The opera is approximately two and a half hours long and scored for full symphony orchestra, a (6) six piece jazz combo, 5 principal solo voices, and choir, (approximately 15–20 voices) plus 6–7 ballet dancers. The overture presents a formidable melange of jazz voicings which tend to appear in a supporting role in the lower brass, namely the trombones and french horns. The violins tend to play a more traditional role by playing in a typical legato style and very rarely play in a jazz rhythmic mode as do the trumpets and woodwinds. Hall's Aria, which appears at the very end of the opera, is presented in a traditional jazz eight (8) bar setting. The harmonic structure is in many ways reminiscent of the typical jazz standard ballad.

The melody is rhythmically simple and tends to be scalar in motion. What is interesting about working in this manner is the fact that I, together with many of my younger colleagues who also compose in this tradition, make a conscious effort to integrate the two disciplines (Jazz and Western European Art music) in an even manner. Thus we find that both the Jazz and Western European Art music traditions are meticulously merged together resulting in the creation of a cohesive and balanced tonal unit. In the case of many of the earlier African American composers who composed in the Western European Art tradition, the Western classical or art tradition tended to dominate the composition.

Another African American composer who borrows from his jazz experience to compose classical music is **Jimmy Heath.** Heath, a tenor saxophonist, composer and teacher, has performed with some of the greatest musicians of our time: Dizzy Gillespie, Miles Davis, Coleman Hawkins, Errol Garner, John Coltrane, Max Roach and Charlie Parker, among others. He has won a number of outstanding awards and is also recognized by his peers as one of jazz's premiere arrangers. In 1980, Heath received a Grammy nomination for a recording entitled "Live at the Public Theater—Featuring The Heath Brothers" on Columbia Records and has recorded numerous subsequent albums. Heath also received an honorary doctorate from Sojourner Douglass College in Baltimore, Maryland in 1985 and is currently on the faculty at Queens College in Brooklyn, New York.

Heath's work consists of standard jazz classics as well as works that focus on Western classical compositional techniques. He was commissioned by the Kronos String Quartet to orchestrate John Coltrane's *Naima* for performance on one of their cross-country tours. According to Jimmy, the work presented several problems primarily because none of the members of the Kronos String Quartet actually could improvise in a jazz style or mode. This presented the

Jimmy Heath. Courtesy of Mitchell Seidel.

special challenge of incorporating an improvised solo of John Coltrane's into the composition and assimilating the solo into an originally-composed improvisation already present in the body of the composition.

Jimmy was also commissioned by jazz drummer Max Roach to write a piece entitled *Melodic Strings* for the Uptown String Quartet (Lesa Terry, violin [niece of Clark Terry]; Diane Monroe, violin; Eileen M. Folson, cello; and Maxine Roach, viola [daughter of Max Roach]). According to Jimmy, he set about writing a piece with the idea of using as much jazz harmony and form as possible, equally mixed with that of the typical string writing common to string quartets. The piece was to be a part of a recording session that also featured a work by saxophonist and composer Benny Golson entitled *Along Came Betty*. Jimmy stated:

> "After I took the piece to the rehearsal and heard Benny Golson's writing where he used numerous contrapuntal lines, I decided to take my piece back and reconstruct certain parts of the composition. I felt I had used too many vertical harmonies and had not concentrated enough on contrapuntal lines which were very evident in Benny's writing."

Needless to say, this observation highlights some of the problems that many jazz musicians run into when writing for strings, orchestras or classical music in general. Jimmy is perhaps one of jazz's brightest soloists, arrangers and composers, and is considered by many to be one of the true "gems" of our times. However, Jimmy himself admits that he found it a challenge to adapt his jazz background to classical techniques normally associated with string writing in the Western European classical tradition.

David Nathaniel Baker—composer, trombonist and cellist, and the author of several highly acclaimed scholarly books on jazz—is one of today's most versatile African American classical composers. He is currently a Distinguished Professor of Music and Chairman of the Jazz Department at Indiana University School of Music in Bloomington, Indiana. Early in his career, Baker was a jazz trombonist with the orchestras of Quincy Jones, Stan Kenton, Lionel Hampton, Maynard Ferguson and George Russell, and this experience— playing with some of the most highly respected jazz musicians in the world—proved invaluable to Baker when he later began to formulate his own style as a composer. Later, his private studies in classical music with Janos Starker and Gunther Schuller, followed by his jazz-oriented work with George Russell, Bobby Brookmeyer and William Russo, gave him an edge that few of his contemporaries could match.

Baker's ability is exceptional as a leader in the area of arts administration. He is a highly qualified scholar, performer, composer and arts administrator, vice president of the International Association of Jazz Educators and senior consultant to the Smithsonian Institution, as well as musical director and conductor of the much acclaimed Smithsonian Jazz Orchestra, and helped establish the Jazz Service Organization.

Among younger African American composers, Baker is perhaps most unique in his ability to fuse elements of classical music with jazz and African American folk music. For example, Sonata for Jazz Violin and String Quartet is

David N. Baker. Courtesy of Steve Sheldon.

a brilliant work that not only showcases the solo jazz violinist, but presents an equal balance of jazz and classical compositional techniques. In addition, his close association with cellist Janos Starker and violinist Joseph Gingold, together with their willingness to perform his music, no doubt has played an important role in helping Baker to achieve such a high level of competency in his work.

JUST ABOVE MY HEAD
Overture
© Copyright Nathan Davis
Pittsburgh, PA. USA
September, 198

-p.1 Overture-

Fl 1,2
Ob 1,2
Cl 1,2
Bsn 1,2
Hn 1,2
Hn 3,4
Tpt 1,2
Tpt 3,4
Tb 1,2
Tb 3,4
Tymp
Synth
Harp
Vln 1
Vln 2
Vla 1,2
Vc
Cb
Piano
Bass
Drums
Sop
Mezzo
Tenor
Bari
Chorus
Scene: Arthur falls and dies
-p.2 Overture-

A 15
Fl 1,2
Ob 1,2
Cl 1,2
Bsn 1,2
Hn 1,2
Hn 3,4
Tpt 1,2
Tpt 3,4
Tb 1,2
Tb 3,4
Tymp
Synth
Harp
Vln 1
Vln 2
Vla 1,2
Vc
Cb
Piano
Bass
Drums
Sop
Mezzo
Tenor
Bari
Chorus
f
pp
ff

-p.3 Overture-

Fl 1,2
Ob 1,2
Cl 1,2
Bsn 1,2
Hn 1,2
Hn 3,4
Tpt 1,2
Tpt 3,4
Tb 1,2
Tb 3,4
Tymp
cymbal
Synth
Harp
Vln 1
Vln 2
Vla 1,2
Vc
Cb
Piano
Bass
Drums
Sop
Mezzo
Tenor
Bari
Chorus

-p.4 Overture-

JAZZ: Double-time feel
Fl 1,2
Ob 1,2
Cl 1,2
Bsn 1,2
Hn 1,2
Hn 3,4
a 2
Tpt 1,2
Tpt 3,4
Tb 1,2
Tb 3,4
Tymp
Synth
Harp
Vln 1
Vln 2
Vla 1,2
Vc
Cb.
Tpt,Sax
Piano
Double-time feel
Cmin7
Ab7
G7
G7
Fmin9
Bass
Double-time feel
Cmin7
Ab7
G7
G7
Fmin9
Drums
Double-time feel
Sop
Mezzo
Tenor
Bari
Chorus
ppp
mp
p

-p.5 Overture-

Fl 1,2
Ob 1,2
Cl 1,2
Hn 1,2
Hn 3,4
Tpt 1,2
Tpt 3,4
Tb 1,2
Tb 3,4
cymbal
Tymp
Synth
Harp
Vln 1
Vln 2
Vc
Cb
Piano
G7
Cmin
Cmin
G7
Cmin
Bass
G7
Cmin
Cmin
G7
Cmin
Drums
Sop
Mezzo
Tenor
Bari
Chorus

-p.7 Overture-

Fl 1,2
Ob 1,2
Cl 1,2
Bsn 1,2
Hn 1,2
Hn 3,4
Tpt 1,2
Tpt 3,4
Tb 1,2
Tb 3,4
Tymp
Synth
Harp
Vln 1
Vln 2
Vla 1,2
Vc
Cb.
Piano
Bass
Drums
Sop
Mezzo
Tenor
Chorus
Cm Cm Dmin7 G7 Cm6/9 Cm G7 G7+5 Dmin7 G7
Mute

-p.10 Overture-

Ritard
C2
1st only
Fl 1,2
Ob 1,2
Cl 1,2
Bsn 1,2
Hn 1,2
Hn 3,4
Tpt 1,2
Tpt 3,4
Tb 1,2
Tb 3,4
Tymp
Synth
Harp
Vln 1
Vln 2
Vla 1,2
Vc
Cb
Tpt Solo
Piano
Bass
Drums
Sop
Mezzo
Tenor
Bari
Chorus
Mute out
G7
Cm△
Cm7
-p.11 Overture-

-p.12 Overture-

-p.13 Overture-

-p.14 Prolog-

V7 ||: ① I△ VIm7 | ② IIm7 V7 | ③ I△ VIm7 | ④ I△ / / / / |

| VIIm7 III7 | VIm7 / / / / | IIm7 / / / / | V7 / / / / :||

| IIm7 V7 | I△ / / / / |

Hall's Aria- Just above My Head

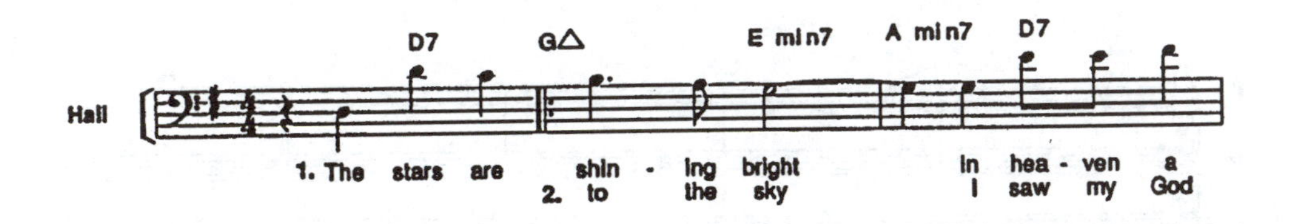

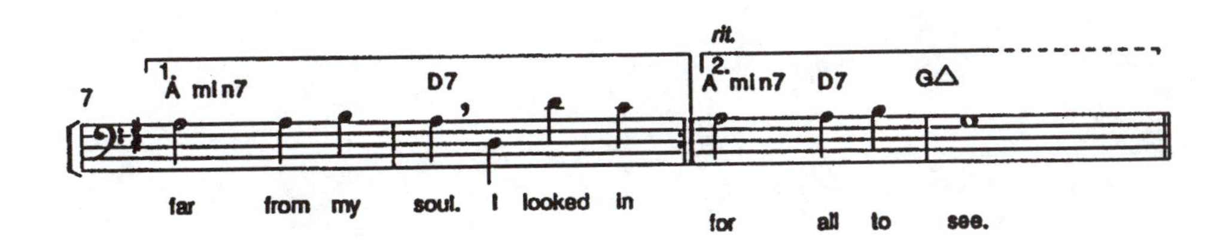

Hall's Aria- Just Above My Head

10 Blues & Rap in African American Society

Blues Form

One true measure of a society's culture is the development of its art. Although technological development may enable a society to withstand aggression and establish stability and continuity as an identifiable group, it is culture (language, art, music, theater, etc.) that assures its place in history. As Nyat Khan states in *The Mysticism of Sound*, "In the beginning there was the word, and the word was sound"—thus music is the ultimate art form. (*The Music of Life*, Hazrat Inayat Khan, Omega Publications, Inc., New Lebanon, New York. 1988) Music is an important aspect of societal growth, and blues and rap music clearly illustrate this point.

The blues, the foundation of rhythm and blues and rock and roll, is a microcosm of African American life and originally served as an accurate portrait of African Americans in the U.S. Whereas early research on African American slaves in the U.S centered primarily on ship logs and court house records, it did not reflect, in many instances, the actual life style and habits of the African American. Early folksongs, especially early blues songs, provided a more accurate account of the lives of the early African American.

The basis of the blues was the work song—developed from the original field hollerer—a melody or musical phrase accompanied by a corresponding rhythm and designed primarily to provide a psycho-spiritual ambiance to help ease the worker's burden. Its purpose was functional as well as entertaining. Today remnants of the work song can be seen in the use of music in major department stores, factories and hospitals, where music is programmed to influence the habits and tensions of the general public. Work songs varied according to geographic area and the type of work. For example, work songs that developed on the southeastern seaboard in Georgia and Florida sound like sea shanties, or songs that were sung at sea. Work songs from other areas reflected logging, picking cotton and laying railroad ties. In each case, the song reflected the type of work being done in that particular geographical area.

As a result, the blues that developed from these work songs were less rhythmical than those developed in the Mississippi Delta region. Regardless of

B.B. King. Archive Photos/Camera Press.

their origins, all blues told the story of suffering and pain; some blues even spoke of returning to the homeland. During the early periods of slavery, the homeland referred to Africa, and later the reference to returning home indicated a deep belief in the hereafter or heaven.

During its early developmental stages, the blues did not have a definite form and was a highly personalized music, unique to each singer—blues could be sweet, cold, warm, bitter, sympathetic or even religious. It was not until four or more individuals performed the blues together that there was a need for a definite form. This explains to some degree why we have so many variances on the early blues.

Blues, without doubt, is a southern African American phenomena. Its acceptance by non-African Americans depended (during the early stages) on accessibility, i.e., the degree of contact between the slave overseer and the slave. During its early development some non-blacks acquired elementary techniques in playing or singing the blues simply by listening to different blues singers on the plantations.

Early blues on the plantation parallels the performance of early African American gospels and spirituals; in fact, there was very little difference between the two styles. Often, early blues songs were mistaken for religious songs. African American slaves, lacking formal training, developed their own special technique of playing musical instruments. The unorthodox sound and execution of the voice used in singing the blues was original and soon became the norm for the blues.

Consider instruments such as the guitar calabash and the banjo. In jazz, it was the banjo (known in Africa as the banjoura), not the guitar, that was one of the original string instruments of the African slave. These instruments were easily constructed and were therefore a natural choice for the slave. Nor was the banjo the only instrument the slaves built. A careful examination of early literary sources indicates that slaves were quite adept at also constructing wooden trumpets, flutes and various drums and percussion instruments. The majority of banjos were three-stringed instruments.

To create the type of accompaniment and background needed to support singing and playing the blues, the African slaves experimented with tapping rhythms while they played, dragging the hands along the strings of the neck of the guitar. This technique is reminiscent of the slap bass style used during the

1920s and 1930s, where the performer actually slapped the bass as he picked or plucked the strings. This style has seen a resurgence today in the thumping style used by young soul and funk electric bass players.

Sound and feeling were more important than technique as the African slave developed more skill in producing the natural sounds of the blues. It was not until after the Civil War that the more widely known Western European guitar was actually used by the African slave. The reason for the distinct and intricate differences between the African slave's instruments and his music and that of the Western European is due to the type of sound produced by these original instruments.

Sociologically speaking, blues and its later counterpart, rap, is a music derived from and reflective of the socioeconomic and cultural experiences of the African American in the new world.

Technically speaking, early blues did not have a definite form. Each and every person was considered to be a blues singer in his own right, inventing a musical story about his or her personal experience. Given the drudgeries of slavery, the subject matter for such songs was readily at hand. Most blues, in their early stages, did not have a harmonic form or a particular melodic structure, but was centered somewhere between the tonic and the minor third.

(During a recent research project at the University of Pittsburgh, students participating in a class in African American music analyzed a number of southern black country preachers and found that the interval of the minor third was the interval most often used during the preacher's sermon. The students then compared these findings with a select number of early gospel and country blues songs. In a number of the early blues songs the interval of a minor third was again the interval most often used. Regardless of whether or not the song was religious, there was an identical approach to the rhythmic and melodic concept being used.)

The heart of blues was its message, and in most instances the message was one of sorrow, or to a lesser degree, happiness. Theoretically speaking it is impossible to separate African American religious music from blues. Contrary to the belief of many African American religious leaders, spirit in African American music does not only refer to religious music. Spirit, in the sense of spirituality or religious sensitivity, refers to a feeling that changes the overall concept of the person or persons in question which after all is the most important concept in examining the origins of blues and spirituals.

In blues we find many different forms. There are religious blues, happy blues, sad blues, country blues, urban blues and blues that talk about the various aspects of African American life. The importance of the blues cannot be overemphasized. As with any other type of folk music its validity is based on its historical development and the role it plays as a mirror of society that chronologically orders the events of a people.

Early blues singers often made up the lyrics as they sang along. Because there was no definite form, almost any subject was acceptable. In the rural areas the singer usually would croon about a broken love affair, problems with crops or farm life, etc. Regardless of the subject matter, the singer would state, in an almost chantlike style, a phrase or line, and then repeat the same phrase again before going on to the punchline or third phrase. There are numerous explanations for the repetitiveness of the first two phrases. The most believable reason is that the singer, unsure of exactly what he or she was going to sing, would repeat the first phrase, thus giving him ample time to think of the final punchline. The first two lines are repeated, and finally, a third line goes on to solve or to summarize the problem. Historians have suggested that the repetitiveness of the first two phrases was intentional and designed to establish a certain rhythmic patter. However, given the spontaneity surrounding the development of blues, this explanation is doubtful. It is more likely that the artist was listening and waiting for spiritual inspiration for the next line. For example, certain country blues singers (and later, urban singers) would sing about a particular problem, then would suddenly insert into the verses: "now you hear me, now you hear me, now you hear me, I said . . . , did you hear me, what did I say?" This technique is often used to include the audience in the singing of the blues, and at the same time it gives the singer time not only to work the crowd but also to develop a theme for the final punchline. Thus the blues singer is cast into the role of story teller or a kind of socio-historian.

How, why and when did form first develop in the blues? During the early 1800's, it was not necessary for blues performers to have a definite melodic, harmonic or rhythmic form in performing the blues. Form was the result of 4 or 5 different artists performing the blues simultaneously, thus creating the need for some kind of unity. This is also true regarding the creation of jazz arrangements. As long as there were only 3 or 4 instruments playing during Dixieland, it was not necessary to have arrangements. As soon as 3 or more horns began to play together, there developed a need for some type of arrangement or unifying structures.

In most instances, early blues singers were men, simply because it was not socially acceptable for women to be blues singers. It was not until the early 1800's, the beginning of the classical blues period, that a significant number of women started singing the blues—singers like "Ma" Gertrude Rainey, Ida Cox and Mamie Smith. Especially during the early years of the blues, these female blues singers were permitted to perform only during intermission at the minstrel shows. The idea of a female blues singer was antisocial and against all religious and moral concepts of that period. They were often booed and yelled off the stage. It was not until "Ma" Gertrude Rainey demanded that those in attendance of her performance give her the respect of remaining silent and listening while she performed, that female singers gained recognition and acceptance.

As the blues developed, form became an important and accepted part of the music, and the form finally agreed upon by most blues singers was, of course, the 12 bar blues form. In addition to the 12 bar blues, there existed, and still exists today, the 8 bar blues, the 16 bar blues and the 24 bar blues which is merely a compilation of the 12 bar blues. The basic 12 bar blues structure can be seen below.

Both the type of work performed and the geographic areas were germane to blues music. Thus, different types of blues music were referred to as schools of blues, e.g., the Delta School, located in Mississippi, Louisiana and parts of Texas.

The Delta School was characterized by a style known as bottle-necking, or sliding of the fingers along the strings of the guitar while using broken whiskey bottle tops, creating a whining or sliding effect. Another characteristic of its sound was the drone, which first became popular with singers like Hudder Ledbetter, better known as Leadbelly. During slavery, the delta region was primarily a cotton picking area. The practice of bottle-necking and the use of the drone paralleled the moaning and whining of the slaves while picking cotton. This transference of emotion from field work to song can be seen as a way of providing psychological relief to the slave.

The Southeastern seaboard produced a different type of blues—the sea shanty. Sea shanties, blues sung by African slaves who were oarsmen at sea (especially along the eastern coast of Florida and Georgia), are associated with a special kind of blues because sea shanties had a different type of rhythm. The rhythm was more suitable for the oarsmen rowing the boats, and the lyrics reflected problems of life at sea.

Another school of the blues was the Midwestern Territory School. Territory blues was characterized by a kind of rolling or romping rubato bass line that became known as boogie-woogie. Boogie-woogie piano players developed their style from a Midwestern type of early guitar picking.

Another school of blues was centered in the urban areas of the Midwest and South, particularly Chicago, Kansas City and Memphis. These cities represented the "urbanization of the blues"—large urban areas where blacks migrated from the rural areas of the South to the urban areas of the North. The blues is primarily a southern phenomenon that developed in the rural areas of the South and eventually found its way to the urban areas of the North with the migration of the country blues singers. Between 1910 and 1920, as African Americans migrated from the rural areas of the South to the urban areas of the North, major blues areas developed in the northern cities like Chicago, Buffalo, Kansas City and St. Louis in the Midwest.

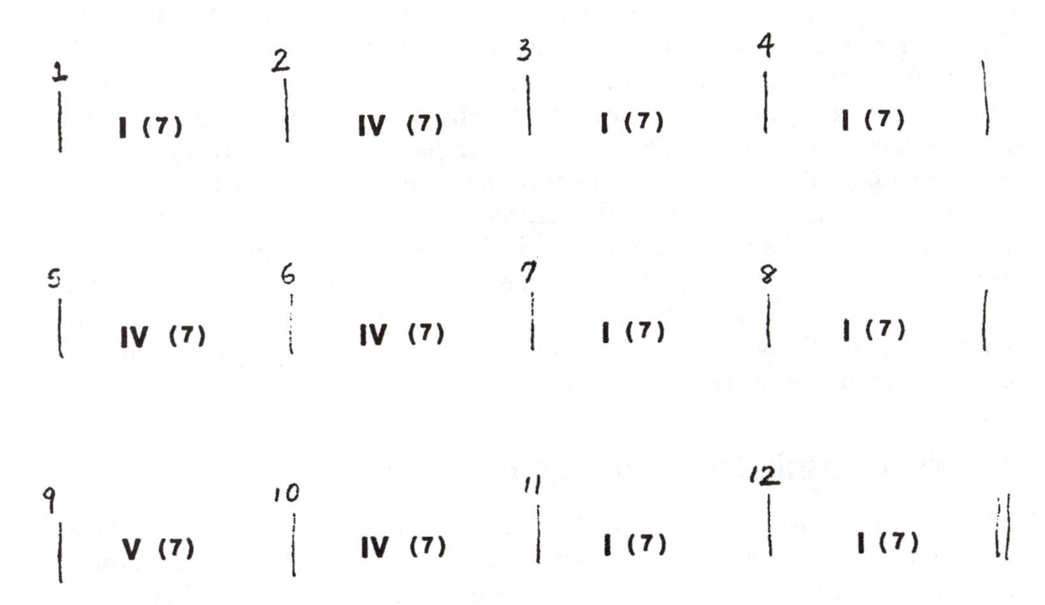

(I remember once going to New Orleans and announcing that I was going to play some "real" Kansas City Blues. I then stated that because I was from Kansas City, I felt I had a special way of playing the blues. At that point, Charlie Bering, the owner of the club Lou's & Charlie's, whispered to me: "Be careful what you say down here in New Orleans because people down here feel that they started the blues! They had a lot to do with it so, you gotta be careful what you say." As we started to play, I found that the New Orleaneans began to participate and they indeed had their own special way of relating to the blues.)

During a tour to Birmingham, Alabama, I recall a similar situation where local musicians explained to me that they, too, had a special way of singing and performing the blues. (Other cities like Dallas-Houston, Texas and Jackson, Mississippi make similar claims.) So, in almost every major city in the United States, you will find a special kind of reaction to the blues that is germane to that particular geographical area.

Some of the more influential male blues singers include not only Leadbelly, but also artists like Sunhouse, who, according to Lawrence Cohn (editor of *Nothin' But The Blues*, Cohn, Lawrence, New York: Abbeville Press, one of the most comprehensive studies on the blues ever published in the United States), was one of the most important blues artists of our time. Another prominent male figure in blues was W.C. Handy, the first person to publish the blues and who is considered to be the father of the blues. Handy composed the two most popular blues compositions of his time: *Memphis Blues* and *St. Louis Blues*. Other important male blues figures, according to Cohn, include Charlie Patton, Lightnin Hopkins, Howlin Wolf, Robert Townsend, Blind Lemon Jefferson, Muddy Waters and Memphis Slim (aka Peter Chapman).

Blues Women

There were also a number of women involved in the development of the blues. Two of the most influential and important female blues singers were "Ma" Gertrude Rainey and Mamie Smith. With her recording of *Crazy Blues* in 1920, Mamie Smith showed the American public that there was a real market for blues recordings. Other important female blues singers who pioneered the singing of blues include Trixie Smith, Ida Cox, Sarah Martin, Sippie Wallace, Victoria Spivey and Alberta Hunter. These women were known as Classical Blues Singers.

Classical blues was a period that primarily focused on women in the blues. Many women in the south had a very difficult time obtaining work as blues singers because it was not safe for women to travel—especially because the blues was considered to be the "devil's music." Some of the difficulty encountered in the south by female blues singers was because of people's prejudice against women performers.

The Relationship between Jazz and the Blues

While friction exists between vocalists and instrumentalists in jazz, it is even more evident in the blues. Many instrumentalists, especially successful ones, tend to deny this division. However, vocalists who sang in bands headed by

Ma Rainey. Archive Photos/Frank Driggs Collection.

instrumentalists will attest to the competitive tensions. The division occurs as vocalists become more popular and end up commanding more money than their instrumental counterparts. This is primarily due to the close rapport that vocalists often develop with the audience. This closeness can be attributed to the fact that vocalists use words to interpret songs while the instrumentalist is limited to the use of notes. The audience may feel more comfortable with the vocalist because of this, creating a stronger bond between vocalist and audience. Thus the vocalists were able to win the approval of audiences more rapidly than instrumentalists. In most instances, the instrumentalists or band leaders were responsible for providing the initial platform for the talents of the vocalist. Thus, a professional jealousy develops when the vocalist becomes a superstar, sometimes overshadowing the efforts of the instrumentalist.

Many blues artists, because of the simplicity of their music and the enormous possibility for crossover (or the ability to attract a wider audience), tend to become very popular and successful. The jazz musician who has practiced his art and continues to practice his art, finds himself in a position of being left behind. This is not a new development. It has always existed. One of the myths concerning this problem is that once the artist gains acceptance, he somehow loses his ability to play true jazz. This assumption is absolutely ridiculous. Once an artist has established a certain technique and ability, given a normal amount of practice and performance, etc., that ability remains. However, the more important issues are; What is blues? What is jazz? Are the two the same and who is responsible for deciding what is good/bad/valid or invalid?

In African American music, the ingredients that make up the origins of blues are identical to those of jazz. These include the use of blue notes; anticipation and delay; tone coloration and timbre; bends and slides; and call and response form. If both blues and jazz developed from the same source, exactly when did blues and jazz begin to separate, if they did in fact separate at all? It was not until jazz and blues moved to the cities during the early 1900's that we find the separation becoming more evident.

Most historians identify the early 1900s as the period when blues became more closely aligned to jazz. Earlier blues performers and the jazz performer were, in most instances, one and the same. In fact, W.C. Handy, often referred to as the "Father of the Blues" was a Ragtime and Dixieland cornet player. The fact that he is listed in all three areas should shed some light on the musical homogeneity of jazz and blues.

The division of blues and jazz was nurtured by the music industry in an attempt to sell more records by creating larger markets. The first African American owned record company in the United States, Black Swan Records, concentrated on blues singers like Ethel Waters. Other record companies involved in producing earlier blues included Q.R.S., OKeh, Columbia, Paramount, Victor, Vocalion, Bluebird and Decca Records. (Cohn, Lawrence, *Nothin' But The Blues*)

When the major record companies found that they could make more money by targeting the blues audience separate from the jazz audience, they did just that. From the beginnings of the blues, a certain segment of the population, non-supporters of blues, felt the blues was the devil's music and should be avoided. Because of this, certain major record companies targeted these people, hoping to stimulate more sales. During the 1920s, blues singers enjoyed enormous success, some of it due to the promotion from record companies. As time progressed, the blues singer generally was marketed more successfully than the jazz musician. Quite naturally, this created a division between the two performers (the blues singer and the jazz musician). To some degree this division exists even today.

It is amazing that the blues revolution of the 1960s brought blues and pop musicians back to jazz. Young Europeans and European Americans who embraced African American music in the form of rock wanted to trace the origins of the rock genre. Groups like Blood, Sweat & Tears and Chicago (with jazz artists like trumpeter Lew Soloff and alto saxophonist Lou Morinni), were partially responsible for this increased interest in jazz. These young musicians incorporated the styles of Dizzy Gillespie and Charlie Parker into their improvisations. The group Chicago used big band brass sounds in their music and fused these sounds together with the more popular rock sounds of the day. The young rock fans who heard this music wholeheartedly embraced these jazz-styled sounds. The brass and rhythm sound, ironically, was part of the original jazz sound of the Dixieland period, when most singers and soloists were accompanied by brass bands. There were also New Orleans Dixieland brass bands that used brass and no rhythmic instruments. This was not a new phenomenon but instead one that had resurfaced after many years.

A more modern relationship between blues and jazz musicians can be found in the music of **Ray Charles**. When asked whether Ray Charles is a blues or a jazz musician, many people are at a loss for words. However, those interested in jazz agree that he is both a bluesman and jazz musician, in the sense that he embodies the qualities of both styles, especially regarding jazz improvisation. Another good example of an African American musician who can be classified as both a jazz musician and a blues musician is James Brown, who also fuses together both musical styles. His band, as well as the band of Ray Charles, has included some of the finest jazz musicians who have ever played. Not all of the musicians are as jazz oriented as Max Roach or Charlie Parker, but they are musicians who can produce jazz of a high quality.

During the 1940s, the split between jazz and blues increased when jazz took an unprecedented direction—musicians played music without a dance beat. In New York City, club owners were required to pay taxes on dance floors. However, a majority of them refused to pay, and dancing was forbidden in their clubs. So in clubs without dancing, the jazz musician was given the green light to create whatever music he wanted to perform. Thus, jazz music was no longer oriented toward dancing as it had been in the past; it became a listening music. Thus the style known as bebop was born. Since blues was a music that people listened and danced to, this division became even more apparent.

The Sociological Issues of the Blues as They Relate to Rap

The relationship between blues and rap serves as a sociological mirror for a particular segment of the population—the young urban African American. As in the case of blues, rap also suffers from a self-imposed division between instrumentally and vocally oriented musicians. Sociologically, rap artists are in a lower musical class than their more musically trained pop or jazz counterpart. This division stems from the same problems that exist between the blues or pop vocalist in a jazz orchestra. The rap musician who delivers a message in a simple and comprehensive manner is likely to become popular more quickly than the instrumental jazz or pop-oriented artist. The result of this general acceptance is that the rap artist acquires a larger following and earns more money in a shorter period of time.

Ray Charles once stated in an interview that he could not accept rap as a legitimate form of music, and other prominent jazz/pop musicians agreed. So throughout the entertainment industry, the questions on everyone's mind was whether rap artists would ever be accepted as fellow musicians, and would rap stand the test of time? While no one actually posed this question to the rap artist, it has become irrelevant since rappers are fast becoming the musical spokespersons for an entire generation of African Americans and pop music lovers. In its early stages, there were even jokes about whether or not the rap artist would last even six months. Needless to say, as of today (1995), rap is enjoying a long and prosperous existence worldwide.

Critics of rap overlook it as a vehicle for social change that bridges communications in a society separated by age, color, politics and economics. Rap mirrors the rap artist's society. As social observers, one of the main questions we must ask ourselves is what elements of a particular society cause rap artists to create their music,—especially when this social portrait is so negative, and are these issues being addressed by the current establishment? While jazz and popular music originally expounded on themes of love, hope and prosperity, rap music is concerned with the negative conditions that exist in inner cities, enabling the rap artist to emerge as the social spokesperson for the African American society as well as other disenfranchised members of society.

The young rap artist, growing up in the inner city, faces daily a life of poverty and rejection in society, a frustrated witness to the prosperous life of his fellow Americans in the media. With little hope for prosperity and an even slimmer hope for any upward mobility, the young inner city youth embraced the music of the streets to ease his pain much in the same way that his forefathers had relied on the blues. As a result, the rap artist created a medium to express his frustration—rap. In many instances, this musical portrayal of life in the inner cities was very gruesome and sometimes brutal and was rejected by both the white establishment as well as middle class African Americans. Many rap artists did nothing to alleviate this feeling of betrayal and mistrust. Instead, some of the more daring young rappers added to this frustration by performing songs that not only portrayed an evil and unjust society, but also showed a strong disregard for civil obedience and family values—thus, the introduction of gangsta rap.

The apex of this frustration and mistrust between artist and audience came with the introduction of rap songs which called for the annihilation of law enforcement officers. This open hostility toward certain segments of society, together with the accelerated gang activity primarily within the African American community, provided a platform for many young rap artists seeking easy ways to enter into the music business. Young rappers, however, in their attempt to gain accessibility to the market, were no more hostile or anti-social than their earlier blues predecessors. They were trying to capitalize on the sudden popularity of rap in order to gain entrance into the lucrative record market that existed for young African Americans.

Shortly after gangsta rap began to infiltrate the airwaves, a strong anti-rap movement arose in the United States. A committee headed by "Tipper" Gore (wife of U.S. Vice President, Al Gore) asked Congress to pass a bill calling for the censorship and labeling of records that used crude and unsanctioned language. Advocates of free speech, the American Civil Liberties Union and other similar organizations protested because of the infringement on the basic right of freedom of speech. The question then became, How responsible is the artist, and the record companies who produced these artists, for the violence that exists in society? Is violence indeed spurred on by the lyrics or prose of the rap artist or is it merely an aftermath or reflection of what already exists in society? In response to these questions, rap artists have stated that they were merely expressing what already existed. However, there were also those artists who stated that they were simply warning society about what was inevitable and what was surely to come about if certain actions were not taken to correct the ills found in society.

These events are interesting because for the first time, there is a sincere heightened awareness among the general public and the music industry concerning the ability of art to influence society. Whether or not it is right or wrong to censor music, art, writings, etc., will probably always remain a question in the minds of many civil libertarians, but the fact remains, there exists a certain amount of responsibility among all citizens for the safety and well being of its citizenry. This should be the primary concern of a society regardless of its financial success, political conviction or religion. However, in many instances, this is not the case. The goal of a large number of artists, record companies and their managers is financial gain at any cost.

One of the brighter spots regarding the responsibility of rap artists toward society is the emergence of a number of new young rap groups who reflect a more positive message. Artists such as Arrested Development, Heavy D and the Boyz, and Jazzy Jeff and the Fresh Prince, saw the negative impact that other artists were having on society and decided they wanted to have a more positive influence. Their efforts appear to be successful. Historically speaking, we have never had a period in African American music that has so engaged the attention of politicians, artists and management in the industry as the various genres of blues and rap groups have.

The early development of rap reflects a cry for social change by inner-city African American youth. The recordings of artists like Run DMC, Public Enemy, LL Cool J, M.C Hammer and Ice T. have alerted society to the injustices that pit brother against brother and nations against their inhabitants. Rap has served the same purpose during the 1970s to 1990s that the blues had earlier—as a reflection of the ills and misfortunes of the African American's plight in American society.

Although rap gained its popularity during the 1970s, its roots date back to the 1940s and 1950s when African American youth gathered on urban street corners to sing acappella and participate in "rap" sessions. These sessions, in which young African Americans talked "jive" to each other, told a story about an event or crisis that had affected the storyteller. The stories were revealed in a rhythmic and poetic manner, and always in a provocative and suggestive way.

Rap is not the first time that music has communicated the feelings of an oppressed people. Throughout history, music has expressed social, political and spiritual feelings. Why then, has rap been singled out as the "bad boy" of the music world? Perhaps its message is too frightening—the irresistible combination of music, poetry and rhythm has had too powerful an impact on society.

One major difference between rap and the blues is geography. Rap originated in the overcrowded, depressed urban areas of New York City (predominately in the South Bronx and Harlem), whereas the blues began in the humble surroundings of the rural south. However, the lyrics that speak of the disenfranchised and oppressed, so prevalent in the music of both rap and the blues, also suggest a common social bond—one also found in the folk songs of many nationalities.

Rap began almost as a spontaneous creation of party disc jockeys (DJs) who were hired to furnish music at social events, often as a substitute for live music. In an attempt to liven things up and create ambiance, DJs would scratch the records before spinning them, often talking a little "trash" at the same time. As they gained popularity, DJs acquired more sophisticated equipment and expanded from private house parties to the larger social dances. The new "rappin DJs" style caught on and the more creative rappers began to comer the market; the more jive they talked, the more in demand their services were. Soon, street hip jargon became the measure of rap's validity.

According to Nelson George (*The Death of R&B*), the pioneering rap DJs included: DJ Hollywood, Grandmaster Flash, Kool Herc, and Grand Wizard Theodore and Afrika Bambaataa. As rap gained in popularity, small independent labels recorded rap performers, and in 1979 a group called The Sugar Hill Gang launched what was to become one of rap's first big sellers, "Rapper's Delight." (Note: Sugar Hill refers to a section of homes in Harlem that belonged to upper middle class blacks. The reference to Sugar meant that these blacks were living sweet, i.e., high above poverty.)

If rap was successful with young, street hip, inner-city African Americans, it met opposition within the jazz, pop and traditional African American musical communities. The practitioners of these already well-established forms objected to the fact that many of the newer rap performers were not musicians and had not even considered music as a serious metier until the emergence of the now-successful rap DJs. DJs were taking not only their gigs but also their status as musicians who represented African American jazz and its related styles (R&B, blues, funk, etc.).

Meanwhile, rappers who did not have formal musical training borrowed from the music of established groups—a method known as sampling, in which rappers would record their lyrics onto a background track of someone else's music. This method produced an unforeseen musical marriage, bringing together two unlikely groups: the untrained rapper and the traditionally-trained, jazz/blues/pop musician.

In order to understand rap, it is necessary to re-examine its forerunner—"musical poetry"—because rap is considered both prose, poetry and music. During the late 1950s, a group called the Last Poets upset not only the music world, but society in general with their message of social defiance and (what some called) political insubordination. The language, although sometimes brutal, forecast the social and political climate within the African American community.

Historically, the marriage of poetry and music dates back to the religious song sermon during slavery and the free-style dialogue of the early 1800s known as signifying. Satirical commentary pieces such as *The Signifying Monkey* and *Shine and Dolemite* displayed the ability of ghetto youths to rhyme text; it also exposed a cynical, pseudo-intellectualism that was brilliant. The ability of young, uneducated, inner city youth to memorize verse after verse of humorous, sometimes penetrating, and often politically satirical dialogue, often is overlooked when the lay person listens to someone signify.

According to Joseph Sanford, a University of Pittsburgh administrator, he and fellow University glee club members would compose music to signifying pieces like Shine and then sing them on bus tours. And retired Provost Donald Henderson, at the University of Pittsburgh, used to astound me with his recitations of signifying pieces that he had learned as a youth growing up in Youngstown, Ohio. The extent of signifying outside the black community is unknown; however during the 1950s, it was tremendously popular with young African Americans.

Despite the early resistance of established music and community groups, rap music has made a definite impression on the world. Rap groups, representing all races and ethnic groups, can be found in practically every major music market; there are black African rap groups, Jewish rap groups, Asian rap groups, Spanish rap groups, etc. A large percentage of advertisers in Great Britain and other European countries use rap music in television commercials to sell their products. Rap, whether classified as music, poetry, prose or entertainment, has proved to be an art form destined for a significant place in the history of modern pop entertainment.

11 African American Religious Music in the United States

Although gospels and spirituals are commonly regarded as the primary religious music of African Americans, the variety of styles found within that genre—gospel blues, traditional gospels, modern gospels, southern gospels and folk gospels—rarely surfaces in the number of scholarly works on this subject. Most African Americans have been unaware of a style known as white gospel until television introduced white gospels to a broader audience.

> More than any other group it was the Fisk Jubilee singers who first introduced the sound of African American religious music to the world. In an effort to raise money for the newly established institution, the Fisk Jubilee singers set out on a nationwide tour that conquered the world. Under the direction of George L. White, a young white teacher at the institution, the group of young singers set out on a nationwide tour.
>
> So in 1871 the pilgrimage of the Fisk Jubilee Singers began. North to Cincinnati they rode, four half-clothed black boys and five girl-women, led by a man with a cause and a purpose. (*The Souls of Black Folk*, W.E.B DuBois, Vintage Books, P. 181)

In 1873, after the success of its first national tour, the Fisk group embarked on an international tour of Scotland, Ireland, Switzerland and Germany, raising $150,000 which they donated to the University.

The success of the Fisk tour prompted other black schools to follow suit; Hampton Institute and Tuskeegee Institute launched similar tours that raised a substantial amount of revenue for their schools. This use of musical organizations for institutional fundraising continues today.

The study of African American religious songs dates back to 1867 (some sources date back as early as 1850 with the publication of *Slave Songs of the United States*, compiled and edited by William Francis Allen and Charles P. Ware and Lucy McKim, Simpson Press N.Y.). Other scholarly collections include *Religious Folk Songs of the Negro* edited by Thomas P. Fenner (originally published in 1874); *American Negro Songs: A Comprehensive Collection of 230 Folk Songs, Religious and Secular*, edited by John Wesley Work (1940); and *The Book of American Negro Spirituals*, edited by James Weldon Johnson

Portrait of the Fisk Jubilee Singers. Left to right: Minnie Tate, Green Evans, Isaac Dickerson, Jennie Jackson, Maggie Poster, Ella Sheppard, Thomas Rutling, Benjamin M. Holmes, Eliza Walker. Photographer: Unknown, ca. 1871. Schomburg Center for Research in Black Culture.

(1925). These collections of songs included spirituals, gospels, jubilees, work songs, shouts and game songs.

There was no early clear-cut definition that divided the religious spiritual from the gospels; even today, professional gospel singers, regardless of race or religious preference, rarely understand the difference. Gospels, in their earliest form, were derived from the old song sermon; they also were spontaneous because there was no pre-composed text—only the spoken text of the preacher—which meant that gospels were subject to constant changes. The changes, of course, depended on who was singing.

The gospel usually followed the minister's knowledge of the scripture. Many of the preachers, however, could not read and relied on someone else to interpret the readings and many of the original gospels were based on these interpretations. Spirituals, on the other hand, were based on previously composed Western European hymns, and derived their special characteristics through the Africanization or changing of the music by the African slaves.

Although one of the most controversial questions concerning spirituals and gospels in the United States is the issue of authenticity, in the case of the modern gospel, most religious scholars agree that it was the jazz interpretations by Thomas A. Dorsey that gave birth to this style. "Dorsey, affectionately known as 'Georgia Tom the Father of Modern Gospels,' was born in villa Rica, Georgia. He was the author-composer of more than 1,000 gospel songs as well as hundreds of blues songs." (*The New York Times*, Monday, January 25,1993, an article by Eric Pace.) The term "modern gospel" is usually associated with

Marian Anderson. Archive Photos.

gospel music when the music incorporated the use of jazz/blues-style musical phrases that are often accompanied and supported by seventh and ninth chords.

Many of the early religious songs were often mistaken for blues songs. My great aunt, Madam Ollie Brown, was a self-ordained, sanctified minister of Wings Temple Church of God and Christ who often told the story of the young sinner who was walking alone, whistling a particular blues song. He was approached by a church mother who complimented him on such beautiful singing—that is until she heard the lyrics of the song, which spoke of how badly he had been treated by some evil woman. The fact that the church mother could not distinguish the difference between the religious and blues melodies indicates that, in reality, there was no difference.

Thomas A. Dorsey's interpretation of African American gospels and spirituals was blues-based because he had worked as a blues pianist, accompanying some of the most important blues singers of the time, particularly "Ma" Gertrude Rainey. "I was one of the great bluesmen who traveled the country over." (Nothing But The Blues by Lawrence Cohn, Abbeville Press, p. 134). Of his blues approach to gospels, "I'm not ashamed of my blues" Dorsey told Anthony Heilbut, author of the definitive *The Gospel Sound: Good News and Bad Times* (1971). "Blues is a part of me, the way I play piano, the way I write." (L. Cohn, p. 134.)

Mahalia Jackson. Archive Photos/Frank Driggs Collection.

For many African Americans, gospel music's relationship to blues is a question they would prefer to ignore. The more significant issue is whether gospel music is from traditional African American folk music or western European ethnic music. As for white gospel, it is not only foreign but for some even sacrilegious:

> "Although some of these early collectors maintained, as did William Francis Allen in 1865, that much of the slaves music might no doubt be traced to tunes which they have heard from the whites, and transformed to their own use, . . . their music . . . is rather European than African in its character" (*Black Culture and Black Consciousness: The Sacred World of the Black Slaves*, p. 19).

This is a classic argument used by early western writers to justify the superiority of Western European culture and to support the position of the colonial intelligentsia that anything African was inferior. African American slaves, however, forced into a foreign culture, not only adapted to the music of a different society, but also created a *new* music and culture. William Francis Allen and George Pullen Jackson have both suggested that blacks learned their language and music from their colonial masters. But often overlooked is the fact that the African slaves, unfamiliar with the new surroundings, were forced to change whatever they came in contact with, whether it be language, music,

Sister Rosetta Tharpe. Archive Photos.

art or dance. And by changing the music they came in contact with, they created a new and vibrant original form—Afri-American music.

In music, most scholars agree that a group of notes, regardless of their arrangement or distribution, do not indicate style. Style in music must consider phrasing, tonal color, melodic ornamentation, rhythm and harmonic alterations. Once alterations have taken place, songs, arrangements and even compositions take on a new life of their own.

This "newness" and originality is recognized through the financial compensation to the arrangers of previously composed and arranged songs. This is a recent phenomenon (1960s) that first came to my attention through my association with the German music collection agency, GEMA.

Perhaps the debate surrounding the creators of gospels and spirituals is futile but to many African American music groups the issue is important because a lot of money is involved—money that is not paid to the music's originators. This is another problem central to business practices that relate to the African American artist.

African American gospel music often uses the themes of Christianity and Judaism and many African American churches even have Jewish names, such as Mount Zion Baptist and Mount Sinai Baptist; Methodists, too, often gave Jewish names to their churches. However, despite the Jewish themes found in Afri-American Protestant religions, Catholicism had the most profound effect on African slaves simply because it (Catholicism) affected a larger number of slaves.

Historically, a majority of the Latin American colonies were Catholic, while colonies in North America were primarily Protestant. The Baptist religion most appealed to the African slaves because the Baptists submerged the entire body in water during baptism whereas the Methodists anointed the head or parts of the body. The African slave, predisposed to view water as a form of magic or possessing magical ingredients, preferred the religion that offered the most spiritual (i.e., magical) benefits.

The major theme of many early African American religious songs was suffering. Suffering was the nucleus or focal point that brought two peoples—the African slave (later the African American) and Jews—together. The African slave felt that if the Western God could deliver the Jews from extermination, God could and would do the same for him. From this religious concept sprang hymns like *Joshua Fit the Battle of Jericho*, *Go Down Moses* and *Shalom*, titles that reflect the spiritual bond that existed between African slaves and Judaism.

In early colonial years, a majority of slaves could not read; they learned the scriptures and religious music from their captors. They had no other point of reference. Therefore, any reference to Judaism, Catholicism or Protestantism was a result of adaptation; the African slaves adapted themselves to the scriptures available to them. Thus, spirituals, gospels and other forms of African American religious music reflected the slave's interpretation of the European language, music and literature. Terms like "dis" instead of "this," "dem" instead of "them" or "dere" instead of "there," produces a different sonority, rhythm, and feeling and creates a distinct but related form. In addition, the use of ornamentation further altered the original melodies.

12 African American Artists and Intellectuals in Paris: 1950–1970

During the 1950s and 1960s, African American intellectuals and artists fled the restrictions of the United States to become part of an international avant-garde that was centered in Paris. The views of this elite group often clashed with the Cold War containment policies of the U.S. government, which wanted to prevent Western Europe from submitting to any communist ideology. To this end, the government created a huge propaganda machine to convince Europeans of the "evils" of communism and to persuade them that the U.S. was a capable leader of the western world. This chapter will provide a framework that explains the African American experience in Paris and places the containment strategy of the Cold War in the center of analysis.

The decline of fascism and the end of World War II was also the beginning of the Cold War. With Europe in shambles, the U.S. had assumed a role not only as leader of the western world but also as the main defender against Soviet expansionism. It quickly became clear that the U.S. wanted to gain cultural hegemony in order to strengthen its dominance as a military and economic leader. However, there was one obstacle the U.S. government had not counted on—the artists and intellectuals living in Europe. African Americans, who had settled in Paris after World War II, spoke out against the U.S. as a "racist and less than perfect" society. These statements, however, antagonized the government, and consequently the U.S. felt it necessary to prevent prominent African American intellectuals from making them.

During the Cold War, the programs of "persuasion" of the Truman and Eisenhower administrations were designed to maintain western European economic and military dependence on the U.S. in light of the growing communist threat. The principal strategy which characterized U.S. foreign policy at the time was containment. George F. Kennan, Director of the State Department's policy planning staff during the Truman administration, conceived the containment strategy and was responsible for its implementation.[1] Kennan felt that America's national interest would be served best by maintaining an international equilibrium in which no one country or group of countries could endanger the country's security.

In 1947, Kennan wrote: "our policy must be directed toward restoring a balance of power in Europe and Asia."[2] As he perceived it, the U.S. could tolerate the existence of unfriendly regimes in many areas of the world. Kennan believed, however, that although four regions—the United Kingdom, the Rhine Valley and its adjacent industrial areas, the Soviet Union and Japan—posed a security threat to the U.S. because of their potential military strength, only the Soviet Union combined hostility against the U.S. with the capability of aggression. Thus, the main task of the containment strategy was to prevent the remaining vital regions in western Europe and Japan from falling under communist control, containing Soviet expansionism within eastern bloc countries. Kennan felt that the most effective way to prevent this would entail not only military, economic and political strategies, but also psychological warfare.

Ideology played an important role in the containment strategy. The U.S. government very often perceived revolutionary leftist movements abroad as manifestations of the Soviet Union's expansionism. Neither the threat of Soviet military attack nor international communism was the impetus for the implementation of the containment strategy; instead, it was the idea of a potential psychological vulnerability toward communism on the part of western Europe and Japan. Kennan feared the possibility that western Europeans and Japanese would become so demoralized by the dislocations of World War II and the painstaking reconstruction of their countries that they would become vulnerable to the woes of Soviet expansionism, thus establishing communist governments through communist-led coups or even communist victories through free elections. Since, at the start of the Cold War, most European and Japanese communist parties were aligned with Moscow, a take-over by these groups would have meant that the Soviet Union had thereby extended its domination within Europe and Asia.

Since Kennan saw the problem as psychological, his solution was psychological. He proposed to establish conditions which would restore self-confidence in the nations that were vulnerable to Soviet communist ideology, thereby reducing the Soviet Union's ability to project influence beyond its borders. For Europe, this goal was to be accomplished through economic stability, primarily through the Marshall Plan, a five-year program of economic assistance for Europe.

Several problems arose from the implementation of Kennan's strategy. The main flaw was the difficulty in distinguishing between Soviet expansionism and international communism. The confusion stemmed from the imprecise rhetoric of the Truman administration. In its aim to assure the smooth passage of its foreign aid program through Congress, the Truman administration had presented the Soviet threat in global terms that did not differentiate between communism and Soviet expansionism. The construction of a communist threat reached its climax when Senator Joseph McCarthy began his campaign against not only communists and communist ideology but also fellow travelers in the U.S., accusing his adversaries of disloyalty, even treason.

The containment strategy received the endorsement of the highest authorities of the United States government. In his recommendation of May 1948, Kennan advised that the Central Intelligence Agency (CIA) should use covert political action against communism, the employment of which would be under the control of the Department of State, the Department of Defense and the National Security Council.[3]

In France, the Communist Party was an important and legitimate political party. It had an impressive track record as a significant anti-fascist resistance movement and was a powerful force within the French working class. There is no evidence to support the idea that in post World War II the French Communist party ever posed a serious threat to the U.S. or western Europe. However, the alignment of a large segment of the cultural elite in France with the French Communist Party made artists and intellectuals a target of the U.S. government's containment strategy.

With the beginning of the Korean War in 1950 came a strong neutralist movement that started in Paris under the auspices of leftist groups and individuals (e.g., Pablo Picasso and Jean-Paul Sartre), who refused to associate with either side in the Cold War. They resisted the "persuasion" of the American government's attempt to identify communism as identical with Soviet expansionism. They insisted that they were subscribing to the idea of Communism without supporting U.S. or Soviet expansionism. From the very beginning they opposed the Marshall Plan as a weapon of U.S. expansionism, as much as they rejected Moscow's attempt to colonize eastern Europe.

They organized and promoted the Non-Communist Left. A movement called *Rassemblement Democratique Revolutionaire* was formed to foster a closer cooperation between progressive and liberal French intellectuals and their American counterparts. This was an effort to provide an alternative to the choice between the Soviet Union and the United States as they faced each other in the Cold War. It was this group that the containment strategists targeted.

The Truman Administration reacted to this initiative by pushing a bill through Congress for financial support and transformation of the United States Information Services (USIS) in Paris. The mandate of the agency was to counteract Soviet influence in Paris and initiate an anti-communist propaganda campaign stressing U.S. government initiatives in the realm of cultural and artistic spheres. This was intended to counteract the Soviet Union's efforts promoting Soviet culture abroad.[4]

The "battle for the mind" was heating up in Paris. Opinion leaders were a target for American propaganda abroad. The traditional propaganda audience is the mass audience, but in modern propaganda this is not always the case; often a group of the political or cultural elite of the population is targeted. L. Bogart, in his book *Premises for Propaganda: The U.S. Information Agency's Operating Assumptions in the Cold War* (New York, Free Press, 1976), pointed out that the United States Information Agency (USIA) addressed itself primarily to opinion leaders—those in a position to influence others—rather than to the masses directly. He quoted a USIA report that said "We should think of our audiences as channels rather than as receptacles" and that "it is more important to reach one journalist than ten housewives or five doctors" (p. 56).

Picasso and Sartre, as important opinion leaders for the intellectual community in Europe, did not allow the USIA to use them for these purposes. Recently released documents demonstrate the surveillance of these intellectuals by the U.S. government. The CIA kept files on internationally renowned artists like Leonard Bernstein, Thomas Mann, Fernand Leger, Charles Chaplin and Pablo Picasso, as well as files on members of the African American community of intellectuals and artists in Europe. They kept files even on those leftist European thinkers and artists who were not U.S. citizens and who had never even applied for a visa to visit the U.S. (Mitgang, Herbert, "When Picasso Spooked the FBI," *The New York Times*, 11/11/ 1990.)

It is within this framework that the role of the African American artists and intellectuals in Paris during the 1950s and 1960s must be examined. The most prominent African American writer of the period, Richard Wright, had aligned himself with a group of leftist intellectuals—including Jean-Paul Sartre and Pablo Picasso—who were targets of the containment strategists. According to a number of intellectuals and artists living in Paris during this period, it was Richard Wright's association with this group that led to his becoming a principal target of the U.S. government's containment strategy.

Methods to eliminate the spread of communist ideology within the U.S. had been applied for years. The Soviet revolution and the new society it produced was a significant attraction for young intellectuals in the U.S. Consequently, starting in the 1920s, the U.S. government and its agencies systematically employed all available means to prevent an alliance between the American working class and the young leftist intellectuals with their ideas of world communism. It exercised a form of containment strategy. This strategy included the very tool formerly used in attempts to prevent the working class from uniting in a class movement: agitating ethnic and racial division. Nevertheless, a considerable number of African American intellectuals in the 1920s and 1930s received their initial support from white leftist intellectuals who organized workshops and supported them in finding outlets for the publication of their works. Richard Wright, Chester Himes and many other young writers got their initial start through these efforts. Although Richard Wright and Chester Himes later broke with the Communist party, they never abandoned their leftist fellow travelers, whose ties to the intellectual leftists in Europe encouraged African Americans to settle in Europe. It was in these circles that they were supported in their fight against racism.

When these leftist African Americans attempted to leave for Europe, the immediate strategy of the government was to prevent them from leaving the U.S. by not issuing their passports. In 1946, the U.S. government refused to issue a passport to Richard Wright until it was pressured into doing so by the French government which, with the intervention of Jean-Paul Sartre and other leftist intellectuals, issued an official invitation to Richard Wright.[5] Paul Robeson, who had lived in Paris, London, Moscow and Berlin during the 1920s, was also denied a passport for years during the 1950s. In 1956, W.E.B. DuBois was denied a passport to participate in the First World Conference of Black Writers in Paris.[6] In his autobiography, Chester Himes remembered the irony of the incident when he applied for a passport in 1953. He recalls that everyone who was suspected of having communist affiliations was denied a passport.[7] When time passed and he still had not received his passport, he sent the negative reviews of his novel published in the communist press to the Passport Division of the State Department. He soon received his passport and left for France, never to live in the U.S. again. FBI and/ or CIA files were kept on all these African American intellectuals and writers.[8]

Jazz musicians were the largest segment of African American artists living in Paris at this time. In fact, most great jazz innovators of the period spent considerable time in Europe: James Moody, Kenny Clarke, Dexter Gordon, Bud Powell, Eric Dolphy, Donald Byrd and Coleman Hawkins, to name a few. This community of African American musicians came into existence not only for political reasons but also because of employment opportunities for them in Europe. World War II and the occupation of Europe by the U.S. Armed Forces had exposed a considerable number of African Americans to a society in which racism was less overt than it was in their own country. When the opportunity to work presented itself, many chose to stay.

Although jazz had been forbidden and declared "decadent" under fascism, the "hot" sounds of jazz after liberation were the "craze." jazz symbolized freedom and liberty from oppression and submission and so jazz musicians were among the most employed members of the African American cultural community. Dizzy Gillespie and Kenny Clarke both remembered the exciting tour they did in 1948. During interviews, both stated that never before and never again had they felt so appreciated.[9] Jazz musicians from Dizzy's band (e.g., James Moody) decided to stay in Europe. Kenny Clarke stated that, although he returned to the U.S., he knew at the time that he eventually would return to Paris to live permanently.

The European demand for jazz meant a life of respect and financial comfort for the African American jazz musician. In the U.S., these musicians were often products of urban ghettos, having suffered a life of degradation and humiliation; jazz was considered the music of the outcast. Yet it was one of the few vehicles of upward mobility for young African Americans whose careers were blocked by racism. Through their art they could escape the ghettos. Although not respected by society at large, they found an enthusiastic audience among young, white intellectuals in urban centers like New York, New Orleans and Chicago, the cities which had hosted the birth of jazz. It was as jazz musicians that many of them had the opportunity to travel to Europe as early as the 1920s and 1930s. Bands like that of Duke Ellington and Elmer Snowden had their first great successes in Berlin, Paris and Moscow.

Not only were jazz musicians able to live a comfortable and respectable life in Europe; their music also was respected. In Paris, African American jazz musicians were adored by the crowds, surrounded by the upper crust of French society and invited to their chateaux. They also became part of a group of French intellectual elites that supported African American writers like Richard Wright. Many of these French intellectuals despised U.S. mass culture and idolized the African American jazz musician and his music. There was genuine appreciation of African American jazz music and musicians within the European elite.

At times, French leftist intellectuals attempted to involve the jazz musicians with their political causes. After conducting an extended number of interviews with the musicians, I came to the conclusion that most had been reticent to involve themselves with classic leftist politics. They felt as marginal in French society as they had in the U.S. and were skeptical of the role they would play as African Americans within the context of leftist politics in France.

African American jazz musicians were just as outspoken as African American writers, however, regarding racism in the U.S. They provided the European press with an honest picture of racism in the U.S. To the propaganda machinery of the State Department and the strategists of the containment strategy, this extended coverage of the statements of African American artists and intellectuals was devastating. How could the U.S. propaganda machinery successfully create a positive image of the U.S. that would be imitated on a global scale, particularly in those regions strategically important to the U.S., when the fact was that in their own country 16 million African Americans were being persecuted because of the color of their skin?

African American artists and intellectuals in Paris talked about racism in the U.S., and as well-known and respected public figures, the power of their names emphasized any statements they made to the press. These were opinion leaders. The statements of the African American artists and intellectuals in Paris undermined the efforts of the U.S. government and its agencies to create a positive image of U.S. leadership during the Cold War. Therefore, certain government agencies designed strategies to prevent these African Americans from making further statements.

As mentioned earlier, the end of fascism and World War II was also the beginning of the Cold War. The African American jazz musicians and writers who had decided to stay in Paris became targets of different strategies and tactics that their government implemented during the Cold War. Although the propaganda and persuasion changed from one administration to the next, the majority of the African American artists and writers felt used or under attack. This caused paranoia and suspicion within the African American community in Paris; everyone suspected everyone else of cooperating with the government. In fact, it seemed to some members of the community that this paranoia was, in turn, often used or even created to benefit the strategies of the U.S. administrations.

Unknowingly, the African American artist and intellectual had set himself up. For his retreat from racism in the U.S., he had chosen a region deemed strategically important by the U.S. government. In addition, his statements concerning the horrors of racism in the U.S. threatened the perfect picture of U.S. society and its values—an image that was created for the benefit of psychological warfare against Soviet expansionism. The U.S. government had to consider that western Europeans would not accept U.S. leadership when the picture was darkened by accusations of racism and bigotry, especially when these statements were made by prominent writers and jazz musicians.

However, there may have been another reason for the persecution of the African American cultural community. There was confusion within certain factions of the U.S. administration concerning the implications of the containment strategy that caused strategists to prepare an ideological fight against world communism. The alliance between African American artists and intellectuals with French leftist intellectuals could affect the outlook of the African

American community in the U.S., stirring up a revival of communist ideas. An alliance between African Americans and communists at the U.S. home front had been prevented in a carefully crafted campaign ever since the 1920s. There was reason for the U.S. government to fear that the African Americans would find the ideology and equality that communism offered enticing. Thus, government agencies found it necessary to introduce psychological warfare, and the implementation of the containment strategy in the black ghettos at home.

Threats and persuasion were carried out at passport renewal time, since most African American artists lived in Paris without working permits and/or residency papers. The American passport represented the very existence of African Americans abroad and enabled them to tour throughout Europe. At renewal time, they were all too often reminded that the renewal of their passport was an act of kindness on the part of the U.S. embassy; their passports could easily be revoked. Almost all the African American jazz musicians I interviewed confirmed the explicit threats they received from the embassy at passport renewal time.

There were other ways the U.S. Embassy in Paris intervened to cut personal and intellectual ties between the African American artists and French communists. As stated before, the Communist Party was a legal party with a large membership. Many French jazz fans and musicians were either Communist Party members or friends and/or relatives of party members. Often African American jazz musicians were asked to play for communist rallies. For the cold warriors in the U.S. Embassy, this must have been a constant annoyance. They often found ways to warn the jazz musicians that it was not advisable to play for a particular rally. Some of the more traditional African American jazz musicians who did not want to risk heightening hostility from U.S. government agencies reluctantly complied with these threats, others openly defied them.

Almost all the African American jazz musicians I interviewed stated that they had been approached by U.S. government agencies to inform on the "mood" within the African American community in Paris. Some were even asked to carry documents to eastern bloc countries while touring. It was usually money, "lots of money" that was offered. Another tempting offer was a lucrative State Department tour. Almost all of the African American artists in Paris that I interviewed confirmed the offers they received from U.S. government agencies to collaborate on intelligence procedures. However, they all stated that they had not accepted these offers of collaboration. Yet, the very existence of these offers resulted in acute suspicion within the community—everyone suspecting everyone else to have accepted the lucrative offers. This benefited the strategies of the U.S. agencies. These suspicions had the potential of breaking up the alliance of the writers and musicians, thus making their voice weaker.

However, once Richard Wright became the victim of what everyone suspected was "foul play," these suspicions and fears grew, bordering on terror. Wright's sudden death in 1960 seemed to confirm that his "paranoia," when he had spoken of surveillance and spies surrounding him, had not been paranoia after all.

According to jazz pianist Art Simmons, it was widely accepted in the African American community in Paris at the time that Richard Wright had, in fact, been killed by the CIA.[10]

Richard Wright had been actively involved with the French Communist Party and aligned with the French leftist intellectuals. He had been involved with Sartre in organizing and promoting the non-Communist left. Like Sartre, he had denounced the Marshall Plan and the strategies of the U.S. government to contain Communism. According to his biographer Michel Fabre, Wright never missed a chance to denounce American racism. He repeatedly made public statements denouncing the U.S. as a racist society. According to Fabre, in order to bring him into submission, the U.S. publishing world had started a "smear campaign" against him. The American critics and press turned on him under the pretense that he had been blinded by Communism and had been away from the U.S. too long thus was unable to relate to American life. The most vehement critics included black journalists like some editors of Ebony magazine who refused to publish Wright's articles. Wright and the African Americans were also attacked in an article in Time Magazine "Amidst Alien Corn" (11/17/1958, p.28), quoting from an interview with Richard Wright that he had never given.

Richard Wright did not succumb to these pressures. He insisted that he would have perished during the McCarthy era had he stayed in the U.S. He publicly denounced the U.S. government and its agencies in his last lecture given at the American Church in Paris early November 1960 accusing them of menacing him and placing him under surveillance.[11]

> The system used by America to control American Negroes . . . It is a deadly fight in which brother is set against brother, in which threats of physical violence are hurled by one black to another, where vows to cut or kill are voiced . . . My speaking of this had this aim: perhaps I can make you aware of the tragic tension and frustration which such a system of control inflicts upon Negro artists and intellectuals . . . ("The position of the Negro artist and intellectual in American Society," p.131)

In the same lecture, he went on to analyze the methods in which ideological control was achieved: through spying and through infiltration of revolutionary organizations by black undercover agents of the FBI and CIA. According to Wright:

> I'd go so far as to say that most Communism in the Black Belt today is sponsored by the American government.

Wright went on to state that he had spotted a number of black spies in Paris.

This was the giant African American writer, untouchable in the eyes of most African Americans and French intellectuals. However, two weeks after the denouncement and the open accusations, he was dead under mysterious circumstances.

Rumor spread immediately; of those African Americans whom I interviewed who had lived in Paris at the time, only a few doubted the possibility of CIA involvement in Wright's death. Later investigation into CIA files verified Richard Wright's suspicions: there was indeed an extended CIA file on him.[12] Richard Wright had accused Dick Gibson and even writer William Gardener Smith of having been informers for the CIA, keeping him under surveillance.[13] This prompted LeRoy S. Hodges, Jr. to state that there was even suspicion of Richard Wright having been a CIA informer.[14] It is known that he accepted money from some U.S. cultural agencies and foundations to travel to Third World countries. However, according to Michel Fabre, when these agencies had tried to dictate the subjects on which he could write, he had rejected the funds. According to Fabre, Wright even went to the Bandung Conference on CIA money, but no censorship was imposed.

The point is not who was informing on whom but rather the extended CIA and FBI files on Richard Wright, William Gardener Smith, Chester Himes, James Baldwin and many others.[15] What is also important is the psychological effect the sudden death of Richard Wright had on the African American community in Paris. Their perception was that if the U.S. government would not hesitate to eliminate a world figure like Richard Wright then there was little doubt that it would not hesitate to eliminate any one of them. Fear and paranoia grew to new heights in the African American community.

The early 1960s brought President Kennedy into the White House and new hope was expressed within the African American community. However, the Kennedy administration continued the containment strategy, emphasizing U.S. propaganda, especially on the cultural front. Programs were designed to more vigorously support the arts. The President himself promised a partnership between the government and the artistic community, particularly abroad. Kennedy's aim seem to have been to change the opinion of the European elite, which regarded the U.S. as an intellectual and artistic wasteland.

The Kennedy administration used the American avant-garde artists in its cultural propaganda strategies abroad and it more effectively used jazz, the indigenous music of America. Most of the cultural elites, especially in Europe had embraced jazz as one of the few true American art forms. Kennedy's policies on the cultural front were supported by the avant-garde elite, who regarded these policies as progressive.

As former administrations had done in a more limited form, the Kennedy administration tempted the African American jazz musician with lucrative State Department tours promoting the indigenous American music, jazz. The African American jazz musicians traveled as official ambassadors of goodwill and thus became part of the propaganda machinery to demonstrate U.S. cultural leadership. To some of the jazz musicians this seemed to indicate that things were improving. After all, the jazz musician was demonstrating to the world, in western Europe, the Eastern bloc and Third World countries under the auspices of the U.S. government, that jazz was appreciated as an expression of American art. I remember attending a reception at the American Embassy in Paris given by Ambassador Shriver and his wife Eunice Kennedy, Kennedy's sister. This rather limited and intimate reception was given solely in honor of the African American artists in Paris, most of them jazz musicians. A number of these musicians expressed their opinion afterwards that they were convinced change was in the air with the new administration.

Others, however, felt that Kennedy was a cold warrior like his predecessors. His strategies had changed; a new appeal had been adopted; but his goals remained the same: fighting world communism and Soviet expansionism. Their perception was that like his predecessors he was implementing the containment strategy fighting an alliance of western Europe with Moscow.

By the 1960s, the economic miracle that had taken over Western Europe and Japan, and the rise of a consumer-oriented society, diminished the threat of communism; even the containment strategist had to admit that communism as an enticing ideology was pretty much eliminated. Although the military threat of Soviet expansionism still existed (as evident during the events in Hungary and during the Berlin crisis), there was no danger that any large segment of the population of Japan or western Europe would succumb to Moscow's vows. However, what also became clear was that economic stability and growth reestablished the national pride in those countries and more and more western Europeans rejected U.S. dominance in western Europe, especially on the cultural front. Western Europeans started to reject the U.S. form of capitalism and the impact of "Coca Cola" on their life.

Young leftist intellectuals, especially in Paris, who, like the older generation of Sartre, rejected Soviet expansionism, discovered the Chinese form of communism and began to subscribe to Maoism as an alternative to Moscow's Communism and western capitalism. Mao's teachings became the "bible" of the young intellectuals in Europe. Nouvelle Vague filmmaker Jean Luc Godard named one of his most acclaimed films "La Chinoise." These young European intellectuals had experienced the implementation of the containment strategy of the U.S. government all their lives and rejected the American popular culture and consumerism that had been imposed on them. They saw themselves as connected to Africa, Asia and South America, countries trying to liberate themselves from colonial oppressors and American imperialism. In a number of countries (e.g., Vietnam), the U.S. was replacing the vacuum caused by the defeat of the colonial powers, thus the U.S. was perceived as an imperialistic force.

During the 1960s, the containment strategy was carried out in the emerging new nations in Africa, Asia and in Latin America. Many of these nations subscribed to their own form of communism and socialism, rejecting the models of communism and U.S. capitalism. While some of these nations were encouraged by the Chinese model, in most cases they subscribed to their own individual nationalism, often combining nationalism with their own form of socialism. The tendency of Third World nations to embrace their own forms of nationalism and socialism seems to have been grossly misunderstood by the American administrations engaged in implementing the containment strategy of the Cold War, as it moved increasingly beyond Europe and Japan to the Third World.

The presence of African American artists and intellectuals in Paris exposed them to an international political perspective. In Paris, they received insight into the plight of the Third World countries which were fighting for independence from their colonial oppressors. During the 1960s, while many young African nations were fighting for political independence, the sons and daughters of the Third World elite were studying in Paris. The young African Americans students, writers and artists in Paris who met with these young

African intellectuals were brought in contact with the thoughts of intellectuals like Franz Fanon, and they began to perceive the civil rights struggle in the U.S. as part of a worldwide struggle.

While Martin Luther King and Malcolm X were organizing their national movements in the U.S., the African American artists and intellectuals in Europe were framing the issues of the black movement in global terms, placing the civil rights movement in the U.S. side by side with the struggle of Africans for their independence and a sovereign nation.

Since its beginnings in the late 1940s, the journal, *Présence Africaine*, had served as an effective instrument in communicating the message of the struggle of blacks worldwide. (*Presence Africaine* "La Communauté noire americaine et la révolution africaine, 2ème, 1965, p.37ff and *Présence Africaine* "Programme de L'Organisation de L'Unité Afro Americaine, 2ème, 1967, p.70ff) W.E.B. DuBois had been one of the fathers of the Pan-African movement and Richard Wright had dedicated many works to the struggle for African independence. In the 1950s, Richard Wright had been the leader of the African American intellectuals and artists in Paris, aligned with the African elite as well as with the French leftist intellectuals.

During the 1960s, after Richard Wright's death, Chester Himes replaced Wright at the center of the African American avant-garde. In a way very different from Wright, Himes was instrumental in shaping the thought of the African American artists and intellectuals. Although a wanderer and a loner, Himes dominated the Latin Quarter of the 1960s. He had found the right tone to address the predominantly male community of African Americans in Paris— not only young writers, but also young jazz musicians. His detective stories had the rhythm of urban jazz; he was talking to the African American jazz musicians in their language. While they admired the unreachable Richard Wright and his white intellectual French crowd, the musicians could easily relate to Himes' detective stories, which focused on the madness of the crime world in Harlem.

Chester Himes was a friend to jazz musicians like Bud Powell and Art Simmons. Ever since the bebop period, some of the jazz musicians had become part of the more radicalized political elite of African American society. Chester Himes shared their opinion that a radicalization was necessary because the "man" (the white man) would not give up anything voluntarily, and only violence could bring the U.S. system down.

Most of the African American jazz musicians supported the political agenda of Malcolm X. Many of them also had joined the Muslim movement, rejecting Christianity, which was perceived as holding the black man, worldwide, in spiritual, political and economic bondage. Chester Himes did not agree with Malcolm in religious questions, but he supported Malcolm's political agenda. When Malcolm X was invited to lecture in Paris, it was with Chester Himes, young African American students and writers and a few jazz musicians that he spent most of his time.

Chester Himes and Malcolm X spoke the same language; they both had gone through the racist prison system in the U.S. and they both shared the opinion that the African American had the power to bring the American system down. Yet, they both questioned the political will of African Americans and their dedication to the pursuit of militant actions for their cause. Both Chester and Malcolm discussed with African American artists and intellectuals in Paris the radicalization of the African American cause, the necessary steps to be taken within the U.S. and the simultaneous formation of coalitions worldwide.[16]

Chester Himes remembered:

> "There were a lot of young American blacks in Paris at that time who were devoutly interested in Malcom X . . . Some claimed to be his followers and more or less worshipped him . . . there were scores of black men who claimed to be watching Malcolm for the CIA. Carlos Moore had become very close to Malcolm, translating for him and selecting the people who were allowed to see him. Carlos brought Malcolm up to the apartment on Rue Bourbon-Le-Chateau and left him there to talk to me privately . . . I had talked to Malcolm when the crew from ORTF was in Harlem . . . and he knew that I agreed with everything about his program except his religion. . . . Malcolm had rented the Salle Mutualite on the Left Bank for a series of lectures and the French were having a bad spell of anti-Americanism at the time and gladly rented it to him and saw that he got publicity in the press. His lectures were widely publicized and were attended by hundreds of people. . . . I remember I took Lesley and we saw Ellen Wright . . . There were also numbers of blacks in the hallways who claimed they were working for the CIA. . . . Not a single French gendarme put in an appearance, although a couple of police vans were parked outside . . . I never saw Malcolm again. He was supposed to come back from London the next week but French intelligence got a rumor that the CIA was supposed to kill him and stopped him at the airport and would not let him enter France . . . In two weeks time Malcolm X was dead, gunned down by black assassins in a lecture hall in upper New York City." (Chester Himes, *My Life of Absurdities*, pp. 291/292)

Malcolm X gained a more international view of politics from his trips abroad and his interactions with leaders of Third World nations as well as with members of the African American community in Paris, especially those members who had recently left Paris and had settled in the young state Ghana (welcomed by President Ukrumah and his young socialist government). Malcolm met Chester Himes in Paris, but he met the widow of W.E.B. Dubois and Julie Wright, the daughter of Richard Wright in Ghana. Before his trip abroad, Malcolm's approach had been much more colloquial, geared toward black nationalism within the U.S. When he returned from his tours abroad, he changed his tenor to a more universal approach of solving the problems of African Americans. He began to advocate the unification of all oppressed segments of society, on a global scale regardless of race.

Shortly before his death, Malcolm rallied with members of the young Africans nations to organize a worldwide appeal to the United Nations, planning to bring the case of the racism in the U.S. before the United Nations and the International Court in Den Haag[17]—a step well prepared by some newly independent Third World elites.

Malcolm had wanted to appear at the UN. He wanted the plight of his people brought before a tribunal of the nations of the world. In 1961, Ethiopia and Liberia had filed a petition at the United Nations accusing South Africa of human rights violations. Malcolm had recommended that the two nations strengthen the petition by linking South Africa's human rights violations with North America's human rights violations. Ethiopia and Liberia took his suggestion.

On January 2, 1965, Malcolm announced that his petition would soon be heard before the International Court of Justice in Den Hague. (New York Times, January 2, 1965,6-A) If, indeed, the forces of the U.S. establishment were about to silence Malcolm X, they would have to do so before the petition reached the court and the international media. If Malcolm X had been present at the World Court hearings in Den Hague, no doubt his prominence would have assured that the announcement received front-page headlines in the international press and would have placed the U.S. in the position of being accused of racism—like South Africa—in the global arena. When the story hit the press after Malcolm's murder, it was buried as a minor story inside the *New York Times*. (*New York Times*, March 13, 1965, 2-A.)

Malcolm was assassinated on February 21, 1965, three weeks before he could present the case to the world court in Den Haag. A number of the Third world leaders who had been aligned with Malcolm X were killed or overthrown during the same period. On June 13, 1965, the government of Ahmed Ben Bella of Algeria was overthrown. On January 15, 1965, Burundi Prime Minister Pierrre Ngendandumwe was assassinated. In February 1966, Achmad Sukarno of Indonesia and Kwame Nkrumah were overthrown. (Evanzz, Karl, *The Judas Factor: The Plot to Kill Malcolm X*, Thunder's Mouth Press, 1992, p. 313)

Within hours of Malcolm's murder, USIA began broadcasting stories playing down the significance of Malcolm's role in international politics. However, a number of foreign journalists insisted that they saw the link between the assassination of Malcolm X and other revolutionary world leaders. A press release of the Council of African Organizations stated The butchers of Patrice Lumumba are the same monsters who murdered Malcolm X in cold blood. (Evanzz, p.306)

By the end of the 1960s, the most pressing concern for the U.S. government however, became the growing militancy at home. Jean Francois Revel received great media and public attention with his book *Without Marx or Jesus*.[18] In his work, he predicted that the only possible world revolution was the black revolution and it would start in the U.S. Only the U.S., according to Revel, had the right breeding ground for a revolution: its African American community. This analysis was widely accepted in Western Europe even before Revel discussed it in his work. The prevention of coalitions within the U.S. that would have the capability of spreading revolution, became the main focus point of the US government and its agencies. The impact of radicalized African Americans—who saw the necessity of forming alliances with the white working class in a united class struggle—had to be diminished. According to the Church Committee Report, as early as 1963 the FBI manual had requests for CIA investigations of Americans abroad for internal security reasons. The FBI used the CIA files in the investigations of antiwar activists and black militant leaders who traveled abroad.[19]

By the end of the 1960s, a new group of young avant-garde African American musicians was arriving in Paris and playing "free jazz." Jazz innovator Eric Dolphy had arrived in 1964, inspiring African American musicians with a new concept of jazz. Many young African American jazz musicians who subscribed to "free jazz" followed their idol to Paris. This massive arrival caused suspicion in the community of African American jazz musicians. In order to be a member of the established group, one had to be an excellent jazz musician, playing complicated jazz rhythms and scales. It was not easy to pretend to have these talents and skills. With the arrival of the subscribers to "free jazz," these musicians became skeptical; anything could be sold under the label of "free jazz"; anyone could declare himself to be a "free jazz" musician. A number of the established African American jazz musicians suspected government agents were agents were infiltrating their community under the auspices of the avant-garde flag.

We will never know how right these suspicions were. However, one fact we do know is that these young avant-garde musicians were very politically active. In close alliance with young writers, they organized rallies, forcefully voicing their opinions. They made radical statements, and often their statements were so radical that the group of established jazz musicians suspected that they were CIA agitators, planted to "smoke out" dissent. Their fears were not necessarily unfounded. For example, it is now known that during the 1960s, communist agitators in the U.S. South were almost solely FBI agents trying to spot radical dissent. Thus, when faced with suspect provocation and agitation, the established jazz musicians in Paris reacted prudently.

By the early 1970s, the civil rights struggle in the U.S. remained on top of the agenda and riots against the war in Vietnam intensified. African Americans in Paris felt that their place was no longer abroad because the struggle was now in the open. Cities were burning and they felt obliged to return home to fight the battle which they had helped to agitate.

Notes

1. Thomas H. Etzold and John Lewis Gaddis, *Containment: Documents on American Policy and Strategy, 1945–1950,* (New York: Columbia University Press, 1978).
2. Ibid, p. 27.
3. Ibid, p. 37.
4. Serge Guilbaut, *Reconstructing Modernism,* (Cambridge, MA/London: MIT Press, 1990), p. 60.
5. Addison Gayle, *Richard Wright: Ordeal of a Native Son,* (Garden City: Anchor Press/Doubleday, 1980), p. 186.
6. Ursula Broschke Davis, *The Afro-American Musician and Writer in Paris During the 1950s and 1960s,* Dissertation, (Ann Arbor: University Microfilms International, 1983), p. 177.
7. Chester Himes, *The Quality of Hurt,* (Garden City: Doubleday and Co., 1972), p. 143.
8. James Knippling, *Chester Himes in the Twentieth Century,* Dissertation, (University of Pittsburgh, 1990), p. 90.
9. Ursula Broschke Davis, *Paris Without Regret,* (Iowa City: University of Iowa Press, 1986), p. 50.

10. Art Simons, Interview, (Lester, West Virginia, July 25, 1990).

11. Addison Gayle, *Richard Wright: Ordeal of a Native Son,* p. 298.

12. Addison Gayle, *Richard Wright: Ordeal of a Native Son,* p. 299.

13. Chester Himes, *My Life of Absurdity,* (Garden City: Doubleday and Co., 1976), p. 214.

14. LeRoy S. Hodges, Jr., *Portrait of An Expatriate: William Gardner Smith, Writer,* (Westport/London: Greenwood Press, 1985), p. 56.

15. Ibid, p. 56, 58.

16. John A. Williams, *Amistad I,* (New York: Random House, 1970), p. 46.

17. Karl Evanzz, *The Judas Factor, The Plot to Kill Malcolm X,* (New York: Thunder's Mouth Press, 1992).

18. Jean-Francois Revel, *Without Marx or Jesus.* (Garden City: Doubleday and Co., 1971).

19. Church Committee Report, Book III, 519.

13 The Influence of African American Music

African American music, in its many forms, has played a significant role in changing the sound of music around the world. From its humble beginnings on southern plantations and midwestern corn fields, African American religious music, jazz, blues, work songs, minstrel music, game songs, symphonic works, and operas, have exerted a major influence on the cultural stage, and it is almost impossible to listen to radio or television without hearing some form of African American music in its pure form or some musical—stylistic fragment of it incorporated into today's music.

According to author David R. Baskerville in *Jazz Influence on Art Music to Mid-Century*, (Ph.D. dissertation, Ann Arbor: University Microfilm), composers like Maurice Ravel, Igor Stravinsky, Paul Hindemith and Aaron Copeland all were affected by jazz and used it in their music. Among music scholars, particularly those with an interest in African American music, it is common knowledge that the music of Czechoslovakian composer Anton Dvorak was influenced immensely by his association with African American composer Harry T. Burleigh. As proof of this influence, musicologists and ethnomusicologists point to Dvorak's "New World Symphony."

After the introduction of jazz, especially Ragtime, to European audiences, a majority of composers embraced it, incorporating it into their music. American musicians both black and white helped to spread the word about jazz, particularly composer and band conductor John Philip Sousa.

> "Sousa always included authentic rags as part of repertoire while touring Europe. Almost simultaneously, rags were being introduced in Paris, France where they caught on with a fervor never before seen." (Baskerville Ph.D. dissertation, University Microfilm)

Touring bands during the early 1900s also disseminated the word about jazz and it quickly became the talk of Europe. European music lovers had never heard such an unusual music before—wild, exciting and adventuristic. Jazz musicians were producing a completely new, hauntingly strange, but irresistible music by adding bluesy, ethnic-oriented phrases to almost any form of

The Clef Club. Photographer unknown. Courtesy of Schomburg Center for Research in Black Culture.

music they performed. Europeans were fascinated with this new sound, which contrasted sharply with the traditional folk songs, leider, ballads, love songs, religious songs, saloon music and ceremonial songs.

Just as jazz was a new and phenomenal experience for Europeans, it was also strange and exciting for the African. (I feel that it is important to focus on the European and African continents because of their close association with jazz.) Without doubt, the Europeans, more than any other group outside the U.S., were the first to embrace jazz. It was the intellectually and culturally transformed African American who wove together the musical threads of Western European and West African music into the fabric that formed the basis of jazz, blues, gospels and spirituals.

African American music was not only music, it was a way of life. Jazz musicians spoke a different language, danced a different step, and even acted differently, and the same was true of the African American religious singers. To Europeans, the two groups were the same, representing a particular way of life—the African American lifestyle. Many Americans felt that jazz was distinct from gospels and spirituals and was a completely different music. African American religious musicians, who believed they were anointed by God, refused to associate with jazz musicians, whom they considered sinners. This self-serving hierarchy evolved from the fact that the ministers of the early African American church were thrust into a leadership role within the African American community and it was in many instances these ministers who preached this separation. Unfortunately, this attitude prevailed well after slavery and is even practiced today.

During the early inception of African American concert music, there existed a tradition in which musical organizations supported the performance and advancement of African American music. Some of these early organizations included The Negro Philharmonic Society of New Orleans (1830s), under the direction of Jacques Constantin Deburque; The Colored American Opera Company of Washington D.C. (1870); The Mozart Circle in Cincinnati (1875); The Progressive Musical Union in Boston (1875); The Philharmonic Society of New York (1876); Musical Society of Louisville, Kentucky (1877); and The Pacific Musical Association of San Francisco (1877). (*The Music of Black Americans*, Eileen Southern, W.W. Norton; *Black American Music, Past and Present*, Hildred Roach).

Evidence suggests that a majority of these organizations were predominately African American; however, in areas like New Orleans, some whites were either members of the societies and even musical performers. One of the most popular African American musical organizations was James Reese Europe's Clef Club in New York City. Europe and his orchestra paved the way for the acceptance of "Negro" concert music in the U.S. and Europe. According to author Margaret Just Butcher, he did this by utilizing popular jazz techniques for the saxophone and trumpet.

> "Sweet jazz developed from the saxophone: what subsequently became known as 'hot' jazz stemmed from the trombone and trumpet. Jim Europe and Will Vodery were influential in consolidating these new instrumental setups and timbres in the balanced orchestras. Europe's 15th Regiment Band astounded European musicians, who could not believe that the musicians did not use special instruments totally different from their own. Not until the Negro artist played on instruments borrowed from their host were the latter convinced." (*The Negro in American Culture*, Margaret J. Butcher, pp. 64–65, New American Library)

Jim Reese Europe's role in combining classical music with African American music has often been underplayed, while George Gershwin, the composer of *Rhapsody in Blue* (1924) and the celebrated American in Paris (1928), is noted as a pioneer in the use of jazz and classical music in a composition. As a composer, Gershwin's talent is evident, but the fact remains that the use of jazz as a vehicle for introducing new and innovative ideas into Western European art music was already being done before him.

Europe, to many music lovers, was the "black" Paul Whiteman. He also was a brilliant musician, composer and conductor who was a musical entrepreneur. He organized his own symphony orchestra, The American Syncopated Orchestra, which helped give birth to what has become known as symphonic jazz. Butcher also credits Europe with the creation of the ever-popular fox trot.

"Europe was later to make Negro music the preferred rhythm in the new dance vogue started by Vernon and Irene Castle. As will be noted later, Irene Castle gave Europe full credit for the fox trot, which she labeled the most popular dance of the day." (p. 59, Butcher).

Although not always considered a true jazz musician, James Reese Europe also laid the groundwork for jazz in a concert setting when he performed with his Clef Club Orchestra at Carnegie Hall in 1914. Whiteman's celebrated Aeolian Hall concert was in 1924.) (see *The Encyclopedia of Jazz*, Leonard Feather, a Da Capo paper back)

The work of musicians like James Reese Europe, Fletcher Henderson, Sam Wooding and Duke Ellington was influenced by the Harlem Renaissance. According to most historians the Harlem Renaissance was an era that focused on the artistic and intellectual accomplishments of the African American. While films like "The Cotton Club" portray the Harlem Renaissance from a cultural perspective, little or no attention was placed on the intellectual climate that existed at the time. In addition to the arts, music, dance, theater, literature, painting and sculpture, areas such as economics, technology, politics, sociology, psychology and religion played a prominent role in establishing the "new Negro." Thus we find that the Harlem Renaissance represented a kind of "sociopolitical rebirth" of the African American experience in the United States.

To many, this rebirth was caused by the end of World War I, when African American soldiers came home to a society in which they were denied basic civil rights. Returning Euro-American soldiers also began to question their role in society. World War I had a profound effect; it "disillusioned white (American and European), on the other hand, helped enhance a black self-concept through their own search for valid, authentic experience." (*Harlem Renaissance*, Nathan Irvin Huggins, Oxford University Press, New York, p. 7)

Writers like Eugene O'Neill and Carl Van Vechten encouraged African American writers and actors to establish a black identity, but many Renaissance scholars were critical of the African American's cultural ties to Europe. To some of the more militant critics of the movement, even the music of James Reece Europe's Clef Club Orchestra was too European. (James Reece Europe did not consider his music to be too European; rather, he felt it represented a new voice in American music). Just as African Americans tried to establish a new identity by focusing on their African heritage, other artists tried to imitate European standards and many orchestras tried to sound as European as possible in order to raise the standards of African American music to the level set by European orchestras. Eileen Southern refers to this dilemma of the serious African American musician during the Harlem Renaissance.

> "By 1914 the novelty had worn off: a white critic wrote in Musical America: . . . If the Negro Symphony Orchestra will give its attention during the coming year to a movement or two of a Haydn symphony and play it at its next concert, and if the composers, who this year took such obvious pleasures in conducting their marches, tangos, and waltzes, will write short movements for orchestra, basing them on classic models, next year's concert will inaugurate a new era for the negro musician in New York and will aid him in being appraised at his full value and in being taken seriously." (*The Music of Black Americans* 2nd ed., W.W.Norton, p. 288)

Many African American musicians tried to "please" the critics by making their music sound as European as possible. Even jazz artists like King Joe Oliver and later, Duke Ellington, altered their music to give it a more critically accepted European flavor. Whether this was bad or good depends on how one interprets the concept of what is bad or good. Perhaps a more philosophical approach would be to accept this cultural "melange" as a basis for a new and more exciting music—African American symphonic music.

Again, the idea of a different kind of classical music, an African American classical music, was achieved by implementing stylistic techniques from African American folk songs, blues phrasings, altered harmonies, rhythmic

E. Payans Brass Band, 1884 World's Fair in New Orleans. Courtesy: The Historic New Orleans Collection

syncopation, and the use of instruments associated with jazz. According to Eileen Southern, James Reese Europe accomplished this by utilizing such instruments as mandolins and banjos.

> "Europe pointed out that the mandolin and banjos were used in place of second violins, two clarinets instead of an oboe, baritone horn and trombone instead of French horn and bassoon. He felt, however, that it was the peculiar steady strumming accompaniment of the mandolins and banjos that made the music distinctive, and that the use of ten pianos in the ensemble gave the background of chords essentially typical of Negro harmony. He concluded: 'We have developed a kind of symphony music that, no matter what else you think, is different and distinctive, and that lends itself to the playing of the peculiar compositions of our race.'" (Southern, p. 288)

During the Harlem Renaissance, whites and blacks came together in numbers larger than at in any time in U.S. history (except perhaps for a brief period following the Civil War, 1865–1879). The majority of clubs operating in Harlem during the Renaissance catered to white patrons; blacks were admitted reluctantly. The reason for this was that the owners were afraid that if they admitted too many blacks their rich white clientele would stop patronizing their establishments—thus resulting in a loss of revenue. But for the first time there ex-

Kenny Clarke. Archive Photos/Frank Driggs Collection.

isted an outpouring of interest in the African American and his "unknown" life style. Clubs like the Cotton Club (which at that time had an all white clientele), The Nets, The Rhythm Club, Clark Monroe's Uptown House, Minton's Play House as well as ballrooms like The Savoy Ballroom featured some of the best African American music. (*Black Beauty White Heat* by Franklin Driggs and Harris Lewine, William Morrow Co., Inc.) For many affluent young whites, it was the anticipation of the unknown, the mystery and excitement of going to Harlem that prompted their interest in African Americans. Yet for others it was a genuine interest in learning and experiencing the music, dance, art, literature and culture of the African American.

If the Harlem Renaissance represented the emergence of the Negro as an intellectual and artistic contributor to society, numerous African American musical organizations made such a contribution possible. Musical societies, symphony orchestras, military bands, music schools, opera companies, secret societies (fraternal social groups), churches, institutions and colleges all provided many African American artists with their first opportunity to perform in a professional setting. Some of these non-musical organizations included the Bureau of Refugees and Freedman and Abandoned Lands, who provided food, gave land, and on occasion provided an opportunity for music making. Another similar organization, the American Missionary Association, helped to establish schools and to provide an opportunity for music making.

Secret societies were social or fraternal organizations whose primary function was to provide shelter and stability for its members. They sponsored social dances, picnics, parades and funerals, and naturally they provided music for all of these functions. Although the societies used military-style marching bands for most of their functions, string groups also were employed for events like social balls and private social affairs.

In addition to jazz, religious music and classical music, African American musicians have made a significant contribution to the military brass band tradition. The participation of young African Americans in marching bands, brass bands, and drum and bugle corps is a tradition that is still very much alive today in the African American community. (Excluding participation in the public school marching bands, my early training in music was acquired as a member of the Elks fraternal order's marching band and the VFW [veterans of foreign wars] marching band in Kansas City, MO and Kansas City, Kansas.)

From its very beginnings, there has been a strong African American brass tradition in jazz. The early brass bands of the fraternal organizations and secret societies served as a surrogate family for many African American musicians. The act of creating music together served to help relieve the pressures associated with the life-style the musicians were forced to live.

14 The Role of African American Music in Modern Society

The role of African American music in society is and should be the same as that of any other ethnic music. The fact that there exist distinct differences between various ethnic groups does not mean that their roles are different. In order for the role played by the music of these various groups to be different, their function in society would also have to be different. The results of these variances would also depend on such factors as economics, education, religion, customs, socialization, and to a lesser degree, race.

For instance, a German nuclear physicist who was born and educated in Europe and who has an extensive background in Western European classical music perhaps might find it extremely difficult to understand the traditional music of the Australian Aborigines. After some training and exposure to it, he may develop an appreciation for the music; but to say that he completely understands it would deny the authenticity of Aboriginal culture.

Now if this same German-born scientist actually had been born in the Aboriginal country, raised by the Aborigines, exposed to their music from birth and used the language and its dialects, but received his education in science in Europe, we could assume that he too, regardless of race, would be able to understand this music. Thus, we must also be prepared to apply this same logic to the music of the African American. The question of race is a sensitive one especially when we look at the vast amount of money that is generated by African American music in the world market.

Issues of cultural propriety—such as who is responsible for the preservation and development of the music—are as delicate as racial issues. Ethnomusicologists often ask me for an assurance that they will be able to learn the music of another culture, even though they themselves are not members of that culture or race. I advise them to recognize that cultural differences do not prohibit anyone from learning the habits and customs of a particular group. However, an understanding of a foreign culture may require a set of learning tools different from those for which their training and education may have prepared them. Our own interpretations of the native language may be inadequate, which influences our effort to understand data. Nevertheless, some

Quincy Jones. Archive Photos.

scholars have done an excellent job of chronicling and researching African Americans and jazz music: Alan Lomax, Eileen Southem, Hildred Roach, Bruno Nettl, John Storm Roberts, and Leonard Feather, Leroi Jones (Amir Baraka), Joachim Berendt, and more recently, Donald Byrd and Stanley Crouch.

Still, a majority of scholars interested in black music think of it as only African music. In doing so, they fail to realize that African American music, while a derivative of African music, has in many ways matured and taken on an identity of its own. Songs of sorrow or songs of ridicule have emerged as country blues and urban blues; Anglo-Christian hymns have become spirituals, and the song sermon has developed into the modern gospel. Although African American music is linked historically and thematically to its mother, African music, it is a distinct but intricately related form.

African American folk music is an ethnic music that represents the past experience of African Americans. The music includes forms such as work songs, religious songs (including original African religious songs, gospels and spirituals), game songs, children's songs. In the same way, the earlier forms of both blues and jazz are forms of African American folk music. Needless to say, this does not mean that only African Americans can play this music; it merely points out its correct origin.

If, as E. Franklin Fraiser (*The Black Bourgeoisie*) points out, many African Americans in the Washington D.C. area during the 1940s would hide their blues records under the bed to keep their friends from thinking that they were less cultured, then we can quite accurately predict that those African Americans would probably know less about the blues than a transplanted Swede who grew up with blacks in the Mississippi delta. We should also recognize that a young African American, born in the Mississippi delta and raised on the blues, and who speaks "black english," cannot be expected to understand fully Beethoven's 5th symphony.

African American blues has developed into a highly commercial commodity worth billions of dollars in the world marketplace. It has, more than any other form of ethnic music except Afro-Latin-Caribbean music, captured the minds and hearts of people all over the globe. The only other form of music to approach this same level of popularity is the Brazilian bossa nova.

Folk musicians from Bahia believe the bossa nova to be a derivative of the traditional samba, which is religious in origin. The commercialization and urbanization of the samba rhythms of urban Brazilian musicians during the 1950s, together with modern jazz/pop-oriented harmonies resulted in a new sound that seduced the music loving public the world over. However, despite its popularity and slick commercial packaging, the bossa nova has never reached quite the same level of popularity as African American blues and jazz (although jazz is a highly specialized form of music that appeals to a select audience).

For folk-ethnic music to become popular, the music must be simple and danceable. For example, there are fewer jazz lovers today than there were during the 1930s because the jazz of the swing era was the popular music of its day, while in the 1990s, jazz is not only swing, bebop, hardbop and dixieland, but also mainstream, third stream, fusion, cool and avant-garde. The growth of these sub-group categories, coupled with the emergence of pop-rock music, has delivered a severe blow to the popularity of jazz music. Although there have been other popular forms of music (e.g., country and western and dance-oriented, jazz-styled, big band music), pop-oriented rock did not dominate the world market until the advent of artists like Elvis Presley and The Beatles. (Note: Presley's RCA recording of *Heart Break Hotel* sold over a million copies the first year [1956], followed by eight million records within the next eight months.)

The Relationship Between Rock'n'Roll and Rhythm & Blues

Rock and roll, the cultural offspring of rhythm and blues, owes its name to a Cleveland disk jockey.

> "In 1951, a DJ called Alan Freed launched a series of rhythm reviews at the Cleveland Arena and immediately drew crowds three times the capacity. These shows featured colored acts but were aimed at predominately white audience, and to avoid what he called the racial stigma of the old classification, Freed dropped the term R & B and invented the phrase 'rock'n'roll' instead." (*Rock from the Beginning* by Nik Cohn, Stein and Day Publishers, New York, p. 13).

I also remember feeling puzzled when I would listen to white artists play music normally associated with black performers. For music lovers, as Cohn points out, this new rock and roll music was a "breath of fresh air." At the same time, some African American artists attempted to penetrate the previously all-white music market—by trying to sounding as white as possible. His-

Kathleen Battle as Pamina in Mozart's Die Zauberflöte. Reprinted by permission of Winnie Klotz/Opera News, The Metropolitan Opera Guild, Inc.

torically, this practice dates back to the 1920s when groups like King Joe Oliver adjusted their music from a blues-based, rugged, New Orleans/Dixieland style to suit the tastes of society's dance audience, so that they could get more work.

During this period (which I like to call the second black renaissance of black music), African American artists like Little Richard, Lloyd Price, Chuck Berry, Ruth Brown, Bo Didley, Willie Dixon, James Brown and Muddy Waters

n, George. *The Assassination of Malcolm X.* New York: Pathfinder Press, , 1968.
ck, Francis and Meier, August. *Negro Protest and Thought in the Twen- h Century.* Indianapolis: Bobbs-Merrill, 1965.
, Margaret Just. *The Negro in American Culture.* New York: New Ameri- Library, 1971.
, Margaret Just. *The Negro in American Culture.* New York: Mentor k, 1971.
George W. *Creoles and Cajuns.* New York: Doubleday, 1959.
Clyborn. *Malcolm X: The FBI File.* New York: Carroll & Graf Publish- Inc., 1991.
rian and Britt, Stan. *The Illustrated Encyclopedia of Jazz.* New York: mony Books, 1978.
s, Samuel. *The Bluesmen.* New York: Oak Publications, 1967.
rs, Samuel Barclay. *The Legacy of the Blues: A Glimpse into the Art and Lives of Twelve Great Bluesmen: An Informal Study.* London: Calder & yars, 1975.
, John. *Who's Who of Jazz: Storyville to Swing Street.* London: The omsbury Book Shop, 1990.
an, Robert. *Contemporary Black Thought.* Indianapolis: Bobbs-Merrill, 73.
Committee Report, Book III, 519.
r, Eldridge, *Soul on Ice.* London: Jonathan Cape, 1969.
ill. *Coltrane.* New York: Schirmer, 1976.
an, Peter. *The Liberal Conspiracy: the Congress for Cultural Freedom d the Struggle for the Mind of Postwar Europe.* New York: Free Press, 39.
, Graham. *Jazz: A Student's and Teacher's Guide.* New York: Cambridge iversity Press, 1975.
Mercer and Henderson, Stephen E. *The Militant Black Writer.* Madison, lwaukee: The University of Wisconsin Press, 1969.
r, David Edwin. *International Bibliography of Discographies: Classical sic and Blues. 1962–72.* Littleton, CO: Libraries Unlimited, 1975.
nd, Miles. *Beyond Cloak and Dagger: Inside the CIA.* New York: Pin- cle Books, 1974.
nder, Harold. *Negro Folk Music.* New York: Columbia University Press, 63.
y, Malcolm. *Exile's Return.* New York: Viking Press, 1951.
Harold. *The Crisis of the Negro Intellectual.* New York: William Morrow d Co., 1967.
y Hare, Maud. *Negro Musicians and Their Music.* New York: De Capo ess, Inc., 1974 (reprint).
, Stanley. *The World of Swing.* New York: Charles Scribner's Sons, 1974.
, Jay and Cranet, Elaine. *Living Black in White America.* New York: Wil- m Morrow and Co., 1971.
, Nathan, *Writings In Jazz.* (Fourth Edition). Dubuque: Kendall/Hunt Pub- shing Company, 1990.

were introduced to a new and wider international audience, because rock and roll audiences of the 1950s and 1960s inspired a blues revival that rejuvenated the careers of a significant number of artists.

The music industry quickly picked up on the enthusiasm with which young white teenagers embraced the music of disenfranchised blacks. Whether or not the whites were actually aware that the music was black music is doubtful. There was no conscious effort on the part of white youth to steal the music of African Americans; they were simply out to have a good time and enjoy themselves and they found that enjoyment in black music.

To dismiss rock and roll as a mere copy of 1940s–1950s rhythm and blues overlooks the fact that rock (as well as most forms of ethnic music) is an accumulation of many different styles and forms of music. Rock, especially during the later 1960s and early 1970s, borrowed from African American blues, gospels (traditional, African American and Euro-American) and some types of country and western music.

In the 1970s, many young rock musicians became disillusioned with the lack of technical challenge rock music offered, so they began to study with accomplished jazz musicians. During the same period, I was teaching a summer workshop in Paris at the Paris American Academy, the brainchild of administrator and founder Richard Roy. Each summer, the Paris American Academy offered introductory courses in music and art to young American college students as well as advanced courses for college students and high school teachers. I persuaded Richard Roy to allow me to present courses in Jazz History and Improvisation. After about two years, we began to receive a substantial number of applications from young artists and professional musicians who wanted to learn more about the music of Charlie Parker and Dizzie Gillespie.

I attributed part of this sudden interest to the popularity of musicians like James Brown, Earth, Wind and Fire, Blood, Sweat and Tears and Chicago. In particular, Blood, Sweat and Tears and Chicago were extremely popular with young whites. The bands featured jazz-oriented solos and arrangements but still maintained a funk-rock beat. In the case of Blood, Sweat and Tears, trumpeter soloist, Lew Soloff and alto saxophonist, Lou Marini, were both popular as musicians and exceptional as jazz artists. Many of the young musicians that I came in contact with at the Paris Academy were influenced by these two groups and their soloists.

Racial demographics in the United States contributed to the relationship between rhythm and blues and rock music. According to Billboard magazine (*Inside the Recording Industry*, 1985), the percentage of dollars spent on records indicated that whites spent 89% on recorded music compared to 11% for non-whites. The only area in which non-whites outspent whites was in the area of black-dance. This demonstrates that race can play a major role in the music industry's marketing strategies. The same survey shows that the percentage of dollars spent on rock by whites was 96% compared to 4% by blacks. These statistics mean that rock, a music that clearly derived from rhythm and blues, became a highly profitable commodity once it becomes associated with and absorbed by whites. At the same time, according to the survey, it becomes less appealing, or at least less marketable, to black audiences.

Conclusion

African American music and its derivative forms—Dixieland, ragtime, jazz, gospel, blues, rock, fusion—represent the African American experience in the United States. Sociologically, it signifies rejection and acceptance in societies both past and present. Philosophically, it expresses a search for the meaning of an existence of torment, joy, beauty and finally hope. Culturally, it denotes the influence of slavery on numerous races, religions, nationalities and societies. The effect of African American music on the world establishes it is one of the most dynamic cultural forces ever and its heritage is a unique blend of Western African, Western European (France, England, Holland, German, Belgium, Sweden, Denmark, Portugal and Spain) and Latin American cultures. Just as the African American race is rich in its many diverse skin tones, cranial structures, hair textures, language and other cultural traits, its music also is complex. Our challenge for the future is to identify, cultivate and integrate these many cultural elements in one homogenous unit, one that represents the best of modern man.

Bibliogra

Abdul, Raoul.
Agee, Philip, and Wolf, Louis. *Dirty Work: The CIA* York: Dorsett Press, 1978.
Allen, Robert L. *Black Awakening in Capitalist Am* Doubleday and Co., 1970.
Allen, W. F.
Allen, Walter C.
Armstrong, Louis. *Louis Armstrong: A Self Portrait.* 1971.
Ballanta, Taylor Nicholas. *Saint Helena Island Spiritual* 1925.
Baraka, Imanu Amiri. *Black Music.* New York: William
Baraka, Imanu Amiri. *Blues People.* New York: William
Bastide, Roger. *African Civilizations in the New Worl* Row Publishers, 1971.
Bechet, Sidney. *Treat it Gentle.* New York: Da Capo, 19
Berendt, Joachim Ernst. *The Story of Jazz from New Orl* York: Prentice Hall, 1978.
Blesh, Rudi. *Combo: USA: Eight Lives in Jazz.* Philadel Co., 1971.
Bogart, L. *Premises for Propaganda: The U.S. Informati Assumptions in the Cold War.* New York: Free Press
Boggs, James. *Racism and the Class Struggle.* Monthly Re 1970.
Bornemann, Ernest. *A Critic Looks at Jazz.* London: Wo tion.
Breitman, George. *Malcolm X: By Any Means Necessary.* Press, 1977.
Breitmann, George, ed. *The Last Year of Malcolm X.* New 1967.
Breitman, George. *Race Prejudice.* New York: Pathfinder

Breitm
Inc.
Broder
tiet
Butche
can
Butche
Bo
Cable,
Carson
ers
Case,
Ha
Charte
Charte
the
Bo
Chilto
Bl
Chrism
19
Churc
Cleav
Cole,
Colem
an
19
Collie
Ur
Cook,
M
Coope
M
Copla
na
Courl
1
Cowl
Cruse
a
Curn
P
Danc
Davi
li
Davis
li

Davis, Ursula Broschke. *Paris Without Regret.* Iowa City: University of Iowa Press, 1986.

Davis, Ursula Broschke. *The Afro-American Musician and Writer in Paris During the 1950s and 1960s.* Dissertation. University of Pittsburgh, 1983.

De Lerma, Dominique Rene. *Reflections on Afro-American Music.* Kent, OH: Kent State University Press, 1973.

Dexter, Jr., Dave. *The Jazz Story: From the '90s to the '60s.* New York: 1965.

Dixon, Robert and Goodrich, John. *Blues and Gospel Records 1902–1942: A Discography.* London: Starville Publications, 1969.

Draper, Theodore. *The Rediscovery of Black Nationalism.* New York: The Viking Press Inc., 1970.

Dunbar, Ernest. *The Black Expatriate.* New York: E. P. Dutton and Co., 1968.

DuBois, W.E.B. *The Autobiography of W.E.B. DuBois.* New York: International Publishers, 1975.

Emery, Lynne. *Black Dane in the United States from 1619 to 1970.* Palo Alto, CA: National Press Books, 1972.

Evanzz, Karl. *The Judas Factor. The Plot to Kill Malcolm X.* New York: Thunder's Mouth Press, 1992.

Etzold, Thomas H. and Gaddis, John Lewis. *Containment: Documents on American Policy and Strategy. 1945–1950.* New York: Columbia University Press, 1978.

Fabre, Michel. *The Unfinished Quest of Richard Wright.* New York: William Morrow and Co., 1973.

Fanon, Frantz. *The Wretched of the Earth.* New York: Grove Press, 1968.

Fanon, Frantz. *Black Skin White Masks.* New York: Grove Press, 1963.

Feather, Leonard. *The Book of Jazz.* New York: Meridian Books, Inc., 1959.

Feather, Leonard. *The Encyclopedia of Jazz.* New York: Horizon Press Inc., 1980.

Feather, Leonard. *The Encyclopedia of Jazz in the Sixties.* New York: Horizon Press, 1966.

Feather, Leonard, and Gitler, Ira. *The Encyclopedia of Jazz in the Seventies.* New York: Horizon Press, 1980

Ferris, William. *Blues from the Delta.* London: Studio Vista, 1970.

Fischer, Miles. *Negro Slave Songs in the U.S.* New York: Russell and Russell, 1968.

Gayle, Jr., Addison. *The Black Aesthetic.* New York: Doubleday, 1971.

Gayle, Jr., Addison. *Richard Wright: Ordeal of a Native Son.* Garden City: Anchor Press/Doubleday, 1980.

George, Nelson. *The Death of Rhythm and Blues.* New York: Dutton, 1989.

George, Zelma Watson. *A Guide to Negro Music: An Annotated Bibliography of Negro Music and Art Music by Negro Composers.* New York: Ann Arbor University Microfilms, Publication No. 8021, 1953.

Gershwin, George. *The Relation of Jazz to American Music.* American Composers on American Music. CA: Stanford University Press, 1933.

Gillespie, Dizzy. *To Be or Not To Bop.* Garden City: Doubleday, 1979.

Glass, Paul. *Songs and Stories of Afro-Americans.* New York: Octagon Books, 1970.

Godrich, J. and Dixon, R. M. H. *Blues and Gospel Records: 1902–1962*. London: Storyville Publishers Co., 1969.

Goffin, Robert. *Jazz: From the Congo to the Metropolitan.* Garden City, NY: Da Capo, 1975.

Groom, Bob. *The Blues Revival.* London: Studio Vista, 1971.

Grier, William H. and Cobbs, Price M. *Black Rage.* New York: Basic Books, 1969.

Guilbaut, Serge. *Reconstructing Modernism.* Cambridge, MA/London: The MIT Press, 1954–1964, 1986.

Haas, Robert Bartlett. *William Grant Still and the Fusion of Cultures in American Music.* Los Angeles, CA: Black Sparrow Press, 1972.

Haley, Alex. *The Autobiography of Malcolm X.* New York: Grove City, 1966.

Harrison, Max. *Charlie Parker.* New York: A. S. Barnes, 1961.

Heilbut, Tony. *The Gospel Sound.* New York: Simon and Schuster, 1971.

Hennessey, Mike. Klook: *The Story of Kenny Clarke.* London/New York: Quarter Books, 1990.

Hentoff, Nat and McCarthy, Albert. *Jazz: New Perspectives on the History of Jazz by Twelve of the World's Foremost Jazz Critics and Scholars.* New York: Da Capo, 1974.

Herskovits, Melville J. *The Myth of the Negro Past.* Boston, MA: Beacon Press, 1958.

Himes, Chester. *The Quality of Hurt.* Garden City: Doubleday and Co., 1972.

Himes, Chester. *My Life of Absurdity.* Garden City: Doubleday and Co., 1976.

Himes, Chester. *Black on Black.* Garden City: Doubleday and Co., 1973.

Hodeir, Andre. *The Worlds of Jazz.* New York: Grove Press, 1972.

Hodges, Jr., LeRoy S. *Portrait of an Expatriate: William Gardener Smith Writer.* Westport/London: Greenwood Press, 1985.

Holiday, Billie and Duffy, William. *Lady Sings the Blues.* New York: Avon, 1976.

Hougan, Jim. *Spooks.* New York: Bantam, 1978.

Jackson, Bruce, ed. *The Negro and His Folklore in Nineteenth Century Periodicals.* Austin, TX: University of Texas, 1967.

Johnson, Guy B. *Folk Culture on St. Helena Island,* South Carolina. Chapel Hill, NC: University of North Carolina Press, 1930.

Jones, Bessie and Hawes Lomax, Bess. *Step It Down: Games, Players, Songs and Stories from the Afro-American Heritage.* New York: Harper & Row, 1972.

Jowett, Garth S. and O'Donnell, Victoria. *Propaganda and Persuasion.* Newbury Park, CA, 1992.

Karolyi, Otto. *Introducing Music.* Baltimore, MD: Penguin Books, Inc., 1965.

Katz, Bernard. *The Social Implications of Early Negro Music in the United States.* New York: , 1969.

Kearns, Francis E., ed. *The Black Experience.* New York: The Viking Press, 1970.

Keil, Charles. *Urban Blues.* Chicago, IL: University of Chicago Press, 1966.

Knowles, Louis L., and Prewitt, Kenneth. *Institutional Racism in America.* Englewood Cliffs: Prentice Hall, 1969.

Kofsky, Frank. *Black Nationalism and the Revolution in Music.* New York: Pathfinder Press, 1970.

Krehbiel, Henry Edward. *Afro-American Folksongs.* New York: Ungar, 1962 (reprint).

Kutler, Stanley. *The American Inquisition: Justice and Injustice in the Cold War.* New York: Hill and Wang, 1982.

Leadbetter, Mike. *Nothing But the Blues: An Illustrated Documentary.* London: Hanover Books, Ltd., 1971.

Leadbetter, Mike and Slaven, Neil. *Blues Records 1943–1966.* London: Hanover Books, 1968.

Lee, George W. Beale Street: *Where the Blues Began.* Ballou, 1934.

Lester, Julius. *Look Out Whitey! Black Power's Gon' Get Your Mama!* New York: Grove Press, 1969.

Levine, Lawrence W. *Black Culture and Black Consciousness.* New York: Oxford University Press, 1977.

Levine, Lawrence W. *Black Culture and Black Consciousness.* Oxford: Oxford University Press 1979.

Lincoln, Eric. *The Black Muslims in America.* Boston: Beacon Press, 1961.

Locke, Alain. *The Negro and His Music.* New York: Arno Press, 1969.

Locke, Alain. *Negro Art: Past and Present.* New York: The New York Times, 1969.

Lomax, Louis E. *The Negro Revolt.* New York: Signet Books, 1962.

Lottman, Herbert R. *The Left Bank: Writers, Artists, and Politics from the Popular Front to the Cold War.* Boston: Houghton Mifflin, 1982.

Lovell, Jr., John. *Black Song: The Forge and The Flame.* New York: The Macmillan Co., 1972.

Lowell, John. *Black Song: The Forge and the Flame.* New York: Macmillan, 1937.

Macksey, Richard and Moorer, Frank E. *Richard Wright.* Englewood Cliffs: Prentice Hall, 1984.

McCarthy, Harold T. *The Expatriate Perspective.* Rutherford: Farleigh Dickinson University Press, 1974.

Mitgang, Herbert. "When Picasso Spooked the FBI." *New York Times* 11/11/1990, pp. 1–39.

Mitgang, Herbert. *Dangerous Dossiers: Exposing the Secret War Against America's Greatest Authors.* New York: Donald I. Fine Inc., 1988.

Morgenstern, Dan. *Jazz People.* Englewood Cliffs: Prentice Hall, 1976.

Nelson, Rose K. and Cole, Dorothy L. *The Negro's Contribution to Music in America.* New York: The Bureau for Intercultural Education, 1941.

Nettl, Bruno. *Folk and Traditional Music of the Western Continents.* Englewood Cliffs, NJ, 1965.

Nettl, Bruno. *Theory and Method in Ethnomusicology.* New York: The Free Press, a Division of Macmillan Publishing Co., Inc., 1964.

Newman, Robert P. "Communication Pathologies of Intelligence Systems," *Speech Monographs.* Vol. 42, November 1975, pp 271–290.

Newman, Robert P. *Evidence.* Boston: Houghton Mifflin Comp., 1977.

Ninkovich, Frank A. *The Diplomacy of Ideas.* Cambridge: Cambridge University Press, 1981.
Nkrumah, Kwame. *Africa Must Unite.* New York: New World Paperbacks, 1963.
Oakley, Giles. *The Devil's Music: A History of the Blues.* London: British Broadcasting Corporation, 1976.
Odum, Howard W. and Johnson, Guy B. *Negro Workaday Songs.* Chapel Hill, NC: University of North Carolina Press, 1926.
Ofari, Earl. *The Myth of Black Capitalism.* New York: Monthly Review Press, 1970.
Oliver, Paul. *Savannah Syncopators: African Retentions in the Blues.* New York: Stein and Day, 1970.
O'Reilly, Kenneth. *Hoover and the Un-Americans: The FBI, HUAC, and the Red Menace.* Philadelphia: Temple University Press, 1983.
O'Reilly, Kenneth. *The FBI's Secret File on Black America: 1962–1972.* New York: Free Press; London: Collier Macmillan, 1989.
Ottley, Nevilla E. *Some Famous Black Composers Born Before 1850.* Takoma Park, MD: Classics of Ebony Publishing, 1994.
Parrish, Lydia. *Slave Songs of the Georgia Sea Islands.* Hatboro, PA: Folklore Associates, Inc., 1965 (reprint).
Patterson, Lindsay. *The Negro in Music and Art of the International Library of Negro Life and History.* New York: 1967.
Peterson, C. G. *Creole Songs from New Orleans.* New Orleans, LA:
L. Grunewald Co., 1902.
Pewit Gavin. *Black Music.* London, New York: Hamlyn, 1974.
Ray, David, and Farnsworth, Robert M. *Richard Wright.* Ann Arbor: The University of Michigan Press, 1971, 1973.
Revel, Jeall-Francois. *Without Marx or Jesus.* Garden City: Doubleday and Co., 1971.
Roach, Hildred. *Black American Music: Past and Present.* Boston, MA: Crescendo Publishing Co., 1973.
Robeson, Paul. *Here I Stand.* Boston: Beacon Press, 1958.
Roberts, John Storm. *Black Music of the Two Worlds.* New York: Praeger Publishers, Inc., 1972.
Rubbowsky, John. *Black Music in America.* New York: Basic Books, 1971.
Russell, Tony. Blacks, *Whites and Blues.* New York: Stein and Day, 1970.
Sackheim, Eric, comp. *The Blues Line: A Collection of Blues Lyrics.* New York: Grossman Publishers, 1969.
Sidran, Ben. *Back Talk.* New York: Da Capo Press, 1971
Southern, Eileen, ed. *Readings in Black American Music.* New York: W. W. Norton and Co., Inc., 1971.
Southern, Eileen. *The Music of Black Americans.* New York: W. W. Norton and Co., Inc., 1971.
Sowande, Fela. *The Role of Music in African Society.* Washington D.C.: Howard University Press, 1969.
Spear, Allan H. *Black Chicago: The Making of a Ghetto, 1890–1920.* Chicago, IL: The University of Chicago Press, 1967.

St. Clair, Drake and Clayton, Horace R. *Black Metropolis.* New York: Harcourt Brace, & World, Inc., 1970.
Stewart, Baxter. *Derrick, Ma Rainey and the Classic Blues Singers.* New York: Stein and Day, 1970.
Stearns, Marshall W. *The Story of Jazz.* Oxford: Oxford University Press, 1958.
Stone, Chuck. *Black Political Power in America.* New York: A Delta Book, 1970.
Stone, Ruth M. and Gillis, F. J. *African Music and Oral Data: A Catalog of Field Recordings, 1902–1975.* Bloomington, IN: Indiana University Press, 1976.
Titon, Jeff. *Early Downhome Blues: A Musical and Cultural Analysis.* Urbana, IL: University of Illinois Press, 1957.
Tortolano, William. *Samuel Coleridge Taylor: Anglo-Black Composer 1875–1912.* Scarecrow Press, 1977.
Ungar, Sanford J. *FBI.* Boston: Little, Brown & Co., 1975.
Walton, Ortiz H. *Music: Black White & Blue.* New York: William Morrow and Co., Inc., 1972.
Washington, Jr., Joseph R. *Black Religion.* Boston, MA: Beacon Press, 1970.
White, Walter. *The Negro's Contribution to American Culture: The Sudden Flowering of a Genius Laden Artistic Movement.* Girard, KS: Halderman Julius Pub., 1928.
Williams, Joll A. *Amistad I.* New York: Random House, 1970.
Wise, David. *The American Police State: The Government Against the People.* New York: Vintage Books, 1976.
Work, John W., ed. *Folk Songs of the American Negro.* New York: Negro Universities Press, 1969 (reprint).
Wright, Richard. *Black Power.* New York: Harper and Brothers, 1954.
Wright, Richard. *The Color Curtain.* London: Dennis Dobson, 1956.

NATHAN DAVIS, Ph.D (Ethnomusicology), Wesleyan University, 1974; B.M.E, University of Kansas. Professor of Music, founder and director of the undergraduate Jazz Studies Program and helped establish a Ph.D. program in Ethnomusicology, Chair and Founder of the University of Pittsburgh Annual Seminar on Jazz (this year celebrating the 25th Silver Anniversary); Founder and Director of the University of Pittsburgh International Academy of Jazz; Director of the University of Pittsburgh–Sonny Rollins Jazz Archives; founded the Jazz Studies Program at the Paris American Academy, conducted field work in Ethnomusicology in Brazil, Turkey, Tunisia, Morocco, and the Caribbean Islands: Martinque, Haiti, Trinidad and Tobago. Recipient of the Robert M. Frankel Award by City Theater, 1995 (first year the Award was given outside of the area of theater); Certificate of Recognition for Contribution Towards the Unificaton of the African Community by the Black Action Society, University of Pittsburgh, 1995; invited by the Belgium National Orchestra to compose and perform symphony with orchestra; Commonwealth Fund Award for the Annual Seminar on Jazz; Faculty Award for Composition Grant from the Pennsylvania Council on the Arts, 1984; National Endowment for the Arts Grant which enabled him to complete his "Symphony No. 1 for Orchestra and Jazz Soloist." Composer of the opera entitled *Just Above My Head* based on the novel of the same name by James Baldwin. Author of *Writings In Jazz, African American Music: A Philosophical Look at African American Music In Society;* Editor of the International Jazz Archives Journal. Davis is listed in *Who's Who in America, 1975; Who's Who Among Black Americans, 1975; Outstanding Educators of America, 1975; 1,000 Successful Blacks, 1975; Leonard Feather's Encyclopedia of Jazz in the Sixties and Seventies;* and *Who's Who in the World of Music.* As a professional jazz musician, Nathan Davis has performed both nationally and internationally including France, Switzerland, Japan, Spain, Germany, etc. With a grant from Gulf Oil Corporation, he recorded and produced an LP entitled *Nathan Davis: A Tribute to Dr. Martin Luther King, Jr.* for the annual "Hand in Hand" celebration of Martin Luther King Week. His latest recording, *I'm A Fool To Love You,* can be found on the Tomorrow International, Inc. label.